Sweet Jesus, Is It June Yet?

"I really enjoyed Amy Cattapan's new book! This engaging read certainly resonated with me. This book is the perfect present for any new or seasoned teacher. I'm planning to buy copies for my teacher besties. *Sweet Jesus, Is It June Yet?* couldn't have come at a better time after a year of pandemic teaching. You have a winner with this one!"

Barb Gilman
Cofounder of #CatholicEdChat

"Teaching is tough. The best way to survive and thrive as a teacher is to take the journey with other educators. Amy Cattapan throws struggling teachers a life preserver with this funny and faith-filled set of reflections about the joys of Catholic education. Cattapan is living proof that you can still smile after decades in the classroom, and she invites readers of this book to discover how they can keep smiling, too."

Jared Dees
Founder of TheReligionTeacher.com
and author of *Christ in the Classroom*

"*Sweet Jesus, Is It June Yet?* will make you smile. Amy Cattapan stirs up joy in each of us, sharing gospel passages connected to everyday teaching and reminding us that we are called, we are beloved, and God is pleased with us—all welcome elixirs to the everyday struggles of teaching and of life. This is the book that teachers in Catholic schools need today, but they will also seek it again and again. Cattapan's writing voice is friendly and kind, and she uses gentleness and humor to reassure us that we are called to teach with compassion. I am grateful for having read this lovely book and look forward to sharing it with my Catholic school friends!"

Michelle Lia
Assistant director for the Andrew M. Greeley Center
for Catholic Education, Loyola University Chicago

"In order to thrive in mission, the Catholic educator must have a strong relationship with the Lord Jesus Christ. This dynamic benefits both the teacher and student. And what better teacher then Jesus, the master himself! Whether you are new to teaching or a veteran educator, read this book to enliven your faith, both in and out of the classroom."

Justin McClain
Catholic theology teacher and author of *Called to Teach*

Sweet Jesus, Is It June Yet?

10 WAYS THE GOSPELS
CAN HELP YOU COMBAT
TEACHER BURNOUT

REDISCOVER YOUR
PASSION FOR TEACHING

AMY J. CATTAPAN

AVE MARIA PRESS AVE Notre Dame, Indiana

Founded in 1865, Ave Maria Press is a ministry of the United States Province of Holy Cross.

www.avemariapress.com

Paperback: ISBN-13 978-1-64680-037-7

E-book: ISBN-13 978-1-64680-038-4

Cover images © maroke, urfinguss, and -goldy-, all Getty Images.

Cover and text design by Brianna Dombo.

Printed and bound in the United States of America.

Library of Congress Cataloging-in-Publication Data
Names: Cattapan, Amy J., author.
Title: Sweet Jesus, is it June yet? : 10 ways the gospels can help you combat teacher burnout and rediscover your passion for teaching / Amy J. Cattapan.
Description: Notre Dame, IN : Ave Maria Press, 2021. | Includes bibliographical references. | Summary: "In this book, the author draws valuable insight and practical tools for teachers from the gospels"–Provided by publisher.
Identifiers: LCCN 2021018084 (print) | LCCN 2021018085 (ebook) | ISBN 9781646800377 (paperback) | ISBN 9781646800384 (ebook)
Subjects: LCSH: Teaching--Religious aspects--Christianity. | Jesus Christ--Example. | Bible. Gospels--Criticism, interpretation, etc. | Burn out (Psychology)--Religious aspects--Christianity.
Classification: LCC BV4596.T43 C38 2021 (print) | LCC BV4596.T43 (ebook) | DDC 248.8/8--dc23
LC record available at https://lccn.loc.gov/2021018084
LC ebook record available at https://lccn.loc.gov/2021018085

★

TO MY DAD, PETER CATTAPAN.
THANK YOU FOR ALWAYS
LIVING UP TO YOUR NAME
AND BEING MY ROCK.

YOUR NEVER-ENDING
SUPPORT FOR MY DECISION
TO BECOME A TEACHER
WILL NOT BE FORGOTTEN.

★

Contents

Introduction

I have been teaching for more than twenty years. And since I'm Catholic and guilt would only gnaw at me if I weren't honest, I'm going to tell you the truth: I have thought of throwing in the towel numerous times. This is not the result of any one bad school or bad administrator or bad set of colleagues or frustrating group of students or parents. Over the course of my career, I have taught at three Catholic schools and three public schools (actually five, if you include the two where I did my student teaching). My schools have been in poor neighborhoods, where I had to learn to look for gang clothing; überwealthy suburbs, where helicopter parents ruled; a nearly all-white but socioeconomically diverse rural/suburban neighborhood, where some kids came from million-dollar homes and others strolled in late because they had chores on the farm that morning; and a couple neighborhoods that were as diverse as you could imagine, ethnically, linguistically, and religiously. In other words, I've taught in pretty much every environment possible, and I know that both success and burnout are possible everywhere.

The burnout I've experienced over the years has not come as a surprise. While studying to become a secondary-school English teacher in the 1990s, I heard grim statistics about teacher retention, and the implication was always that teachers quit because they were burned out. In 1997, Linda Darling-Hammond reported that more than thirty percent of beginning teachers leave within their first five years of teaching.[1] More recently, Charles M. Payne stated that 44 percent of new teachers in New York are gone by their fourth year, and about 40 percent of new teachers in Chicago are gone within five years.[2]

Sometimes we teachers burn out because we can't get the funding we need to buy the necessary resources for our classrooms. Sometimes we burn out because it feels like we're working harder than our students, and then to add insult to injury, a parent who is unhappy with something we've done complains that we don't care enough! Sometimes we burn out because we don't feel we have the support of our administrators. Sometimes we burn out because despite giving everything we have, we just can't reach every kid the way we desire.

If you're like me, you felt the Lord call you to be a teacher at a young age, but at times you've wondered if you misunderstood what he was trying to tell you. Some of us went into teaching with grandiose ideas of being the next Mr. Keating from *Dead Poets Society*, inspiring our students to "Carpe diem!" Or maybe we thought we'd be like Michelle Pfeiffer's character in *Dangerous Minds* and stride into an inner-city classroom in a leather jacket, teach some karate moves, and somehow unlock the potential of a group of students nobody thought was worth their time. I mean, after all, didn't Jaime Escalante (of *Stand and Deliver* fame) do that (minus the leather jacket and the karate moves, of course)? Didn't teacher Erin Gruwell have massive success with another group of high school students, with the end result being their book *The Freedom Writers Diary*? Aren't all of us teachers supposed to work such miracles in our classrooms that we get our lives turned into movies in which Hilary Swank (*Freedom Writers*) or Matthew Perry (*The Ron Clark Story*) portray us? Or at the very least, we'll toil for years, and then when we retire, it'll be like *Mr. Holland's Opus* and we'll get a rousing send-off where our former students come back and thank us for the sacrifices we made so that we can finally see that it was all worthwhile!

Sigh. Please tell me you're laughing with me by now.

So here's the question: If we're not all going to get giant pats on the back or have our lives turned into inspirational movies, how are we going to survive year after year . . . often while watching our colleagues become more and more cynical? How can we keep ourselves going when the harsh realities of teaching don't live up to our fairytale-movie expectations? These are the questions I've been bringing to prayer for years now.

The answer seems to be to keep finding ways to reinvigorate my love for teaching and reenergize my approach in the classroom. That's what I hope this book will do for you. As I mentioned before, I'm Catholic, so my guilt won't let me lie to you on this point either. I need this book right now. Over twenty years in, and there are still days when I ask God, "Are you sure you still want me doing this?" (Maybe it's a result of my Jesuit education, but ongoing discernment seems to be a way of life for me.) So I am writing this book to reinvigorate my own teaching and to reenergize my own approach to the classroom, but I think that it will also do the same for you.

Where did I get the idea of pressing the refresh button on my career by reflecting on gospel stories? Well, through prayer, of course. To be honest, I'm pretty terrible at silent prayer. I've never been diagnosed with ADHD, but I swear when I try to pray in silence, my mind jumps around like the proverbial dog chasing after a squirrel. Thankfully, God doesn't need me to give him a lot of silence for him to break through.

In the spring of 2018, I was getting ready to go on a five-day silent retreat at a Jesuit retreat center near Atlanta. (I was going to *force* myself to sit still and listen to God so he could tell me what my next move should be.) Well, God decided he didn't actually need five days. Before I even packed for the retreat, he

Sweet Jesus, Is It June Yet?

made a move. I was sitting on my couch at home, starting the timer on my centering prayer app so that I could sit still and pray.

Moments after the chime signaling the start of my silent period faded away, a thought fell into my head: "Write a book about how to teach like Jesus did." My eyes flew open. Years ago, I was a catechist and a religion teacher, but that's not the work I do now, so I knew this wasn't an idea designed only for religion teachers. This was an idea for every Catholic teacher, whether you teach science or math or language arts or art or any other subject matter! I wanted to look at how we could follow Christ's example and lessons from the gospels as we teach from day to day. Surely, Jesus was the greatest teacher in history. Other than ancient scholars like Socrates and Plato, not too many educators can say their teachings are still being passed on two thousand years later. Clearly, Jesus must know a thing or two about teaching. Move over, Mr. Holland, Jesus's legacy is way longer-lasting!

And he definitely knew a thing or two about teaching under difficult circumstances. He was so rejected in his own hometown that they chased him out of Nazareth with plans to hurl him off a cliff (see Luke 4:16–30). Even when he did something good like releasing men from the demons that possessed them, "the whole town came out to meet Jesus; and when they saw him, they begged him to leave their neighborhood" (Mt 8:34). No thank-you note with a Starbucks gift card for Jesus! Just "Please, get the heck away from us!" On top of that, the Pharisees continually tried to trick him by asking him questions such as whether or not they should pay taxes (see Matthew 22:15–22), and even tried to arrest him (see John 7:32–36). I'm pretty sure some of my middle school students must be taking notes from the Pharisees on how to trap teachers with tricky questions.

So if you're wondering if teaching is still the right career for you, or you just feel like you need the chance for a little "do-over" at the start of a new school year, won't you join me on this journey? Let's see what we can learn from Jesus. Let's study his life and his teachings—what he taught and how he taught it—and pull out ten golden nuggets that might help us face our next day with the kiddos. In our hearts, we know our kids are worth our time, our talent, and our treasure. But remember, too, that *you* are a precious child of God. He loves you, and you are worth his time. Let's sit at his feet then, and learn from the Master.

ONE

Jesus Began Small

When we get lost in the midst of our daily tasks, it can be good to remember how we started. We have mounds of papers to grade, an inbox flooded with emails, a classroom in need of better organization, new textbooks to evaluate, administrators to report to, and, let's not forget, kids to take care of! It's a fatiguing job that only lets up after the school year closes. Even in summer, many of us work odd jobs so we can pay the bills. I've spent plenty of summers working office temp jobs or department store gigs, or teaching summer school. Maybe some of you even have a second job that you keep all year round. One of my coworkers ran a vending machine business on the side. Another worked evenings and weekends at a bank. A third kept a part-time job at a department store year-round.

While working on this book, I realized that most of the ideas I was jotting down were things that I had known at one point or another, but had forgotten in the midst of a demanding teaching schedule. And I wanted to remember all those reasons I went into teaching in the first place.

Getting the Call

Some of us knew we were going to be teachers from a very young age. My mother would've told you how much I loved school when I was in first grade. I didn't realize it was "uncool" back then. My older brothers might tell you how I used to gather up my stuffed animals when I was little, arrange them in neat rows, wag my little kid finger at them, and tell them that they had better pay attention!

Despite these signs, you should never underestimate the ability of a Cattapan to overanalyze everything and spend forever making a decision. My brothers and I are famous for spending way too much time analyzing a situation. One of my sisters-in-law became so fed up with this family trait that she coined the term "Cattapanalysis Paralysis" since we sometimes get so caught up with our analyzing that we can't make a decision. My decision to become a teacher nearly suffered from CP.

In third grade, I started writing stories. By sixth grade, I had read *Anne of Green Gables* (at the suggestion of one of the loveliest reading teachers I've ever had—God bless Miss Sipiora!), and when I closed the last page of that book, I knew *this* is what I wanted to do for the rest of my life—write stories that touched people's hearts the way L. M. Montgomery's classic tale had touched mine.

A few weeks later, Mom took me to see a musical at our local Catholic high school. I stared, enthralled as these high school kids performed *Guys and Dolls*. When the show ended and everyone stood up and cheered, I thought, *This is what I want to do for the rest of my life—sing and dance on stage until people stand up and applaud!*

By the time eighth grade rolled around, I was back to wanting to be a writer. Maybe it was all those Battle of the Books competitions or my English teacher, Mrs. Boyle, who made me fall in love with grammar (yes, I said grammar). Either way, in my eighth-grade yearbook, I boldly declared I'd be the "author of teen novels." Well, I was right. I've written books for teens and tweens, but that's not my full-time gig.

During high school, I considered becoming a psychologist, but I thought, *Who wants to spend so much time in school?* Even now I want to plant my palm against my face when I think of it. *Duh, Amy. You became a teacher. You're spending the rest of your life in school.*

Senior year, I had an extremely intelligent and difficult A.P. World Literature teacher, Br. Robert Ruhl. He utterly terrified his students. Some people got physically ill before his class and had to run to the bathroom. He never made me *that* nervous, but I would try to avoid eye contact with him as much as possible. He had these steel blue eyes that I swear could shoot laser beams. He was very tall (or at least he seemed so to me at 5'2"), and his body was as lean and ramrod straight as a solid wood plank.

Despite scaring the daylights out of us, he was one of everyone's favorite teachers. The man was absolutely brilliant. He not only took our writing to the next level, but he made us see how some of the world's most talented authors took storytelling to the next level. One thing he did that appealed to me in particular was to discuss the psychology of the characters—*why* they did the things they did and *how* the author portrayed those feelings.

He'd point out a passage where a jealous character ran his finger back and forth across a piece of green furniture, and he'd bark out, "Why did the author make the furniture upholstery green?"

We would all shake in our metal desks and look down, praying he wouldn't call on us because God only knew why the author made the furniture covering green. Slow, awkward, painful moments of silence would tick by as he walked back and forth across the front of the room like a tiger pacing in a cage.

Finally, he would scream out, "Jealousy! He's *green* with envy."

We'd all nod as if that was what we were all about to say if only he'd given us a chance.

I learned so much about writing and books from Br. Ruhl that you might think he was the reason I finally decided on an English education major and not a creative writing major at Marquette University. But nope, it wasn't him.

In college, I had an English professor who spent more time discussing the required topics of our papers than how to write. I was arrogant enough to stare at him and think, *Well, I couldn't be a worse English teacher than this guy!* And that was it. An English teacher was born!

I say this somewhat facetiously because I still hemmed and hawed. My mother did not like the idea at all. In her position as the religious education coordinator at our parish, she had learned firsthand how hard teaching was. Her office was an old classroom, and she often ate lunch in the faculty room where she heard directly from the teachers about the challenges they faced. My mom shared her views with me, hoping to dissuade me. It might have worked if it hadn't been for that choir at our church.

One weekend during college, I was home from Marquette and attending Sunday Mass at my home parish. I remember praying during that Mass about becoming a teacher. Cattap-analysis Paralysis was setting in deep. Could I really make the commitment to a job I knew would be so hard and pay so little? Then during Communion, we sang "Here I Am, Lord." I'd heard the song dozens of times before, but this time I was fighting back tears in the Communion line! All I could think was, *Lord, are you really calling me to be a teacher? Do you really want me to guide your people?* At once, I pictured his "people" as my future students.

And I knew I was sunk. I'd gotten the call. There was no turning back.

I wish we knew what it was like when Jesus got the call to come and be *our* teacher. Wouldn't that be a wild scene in the gospels? Just what might it have been like when God called his only Son to come to Earth?

God the Father: Son, come here for a minute. I've got a job for you.

Jesus: Yes, Dad.

God the Father: I need you to go down to Earth, become human, teach the people our ways—a bunch of them will ignore you, others will completely hate you—and then sacrifice yourself on a cross so that their sins may be forgiven and we can finally open the gates to heaven.

Jesus: Okay, Dad, sounds great!

All right, so we have no idea how this scene actually went. There's no gospel story that explains it, so for inspiration in answering our call to teach, let's look to Jesus's mother.

> In the sixth month the angel Gabriel was sent by God to a town in Galilee called Nazareth, to a virgin engaged to a man whose name was Joseph, of the house of David. The virgin's name was Mary. And he came to her and said, "Greetings, favored one! The Lord is with you." But she was much perplexed by his words and pondered what sort of greeting this might be. The angel said to her, "Do not be afraid, Mary, for you have found favor with God. And now, you will conceive in your womb and bear a son, and you will name him Jesus." (Lk 1:26–31)

A lot of people like to focus on Mary's fiat—her yes—that comes a little later, but I like looking at this part of the story because we see Mary's initial concern. Notice that she is at first "much perplexed" and needs to ponder what type of greeting this is. Perhaps the first time you thought of becoming a teacher, you were also much perplexed and pondered what on earth made you think you could teach. That's okay!

When God first lets us see that he has something amazing in store for us, he often gives us just a little glimpse. Too much at once and we'd be as terrified as Mary trembling in front of a mighty angel.

We might have questions about how God is going to turn us into good teachers. Even Mary questioned the angel: "How can this be, since I am a virgin?" (Lk 1:34). So, too, might we wonder about how to become the kind of teacher God wants us to be.

After the angel explains everything to Mary, she willingly accepts. I had a lot of doubts about becoming a teacher, but when I heard "Here I Am, Lord" at Mass, somehow I knew God was calling me to care for his young children, to hold them in my heart.

Humble Beginnings

If it's still fairly early in your teaching career, you might be questioning your own ability and readiness for this work. My first few years of teaching were filled with the "queasy qualms" (my nickname for the many nauseated mornings I experienced as a young teacher). When you start to feel like you don't have what it takes to teach, take a moment to remember how humble Jesus's own beginning was, and remember that even little babies born in a stable can grow up to be world-changing teachers.

> In those days a decree went out from Emperor
> Augustus that all the world should be registered. This
> was the first registration and was taken while Quir-
> inius was governor of Syria. All went to their own
> towns to be registered. Joseph also went from the
> town of Nazareth in Galilee to Judea, to the city of
> David called Bethlehem, because he was descended
> from the house and family of David. He went to be
> registered with Mary, to whom he was engaged and
> who was expecting a child. While they were there,
> the time came for her to deliver her child. (Lk 2:1–6)

I love how Luke's second chapter starts with Caesar Augustus
declaring that "all the world" must be enrolled. In some trans-
lations of the Bible, this is written as "the whole world."[3] I mean,
the whole world? Really? Well, I guess the "whole world" to Caesar Augustus was everything he had his grubby little hands on,
but still I find it significant. The story of Jesus is about the whole
world. He is a teacher for all the world, and yet he came into this
world as a little baby who was laid in a manger, a germ-infested
feeding trough for horses or cattle. If Jesus can have humble
beginnings, so can we.

My first experience as a teacher came about because of my
mother, which is ironic since she was against my becoming a
teacher. My mother ran our parish's preschool Sunday school
program, which was held during our 10:00 a.m. Mass. I was a
teacher helper starting in grade 6 and then a teacher in high
school.

Looking back on this experience, I see how much it prepared me to teach. I took attendance, planned lessons based on
the provided curriculum, and worked through the occasional
disciplinary problem with a squirrelly four-year-old who was
uninterested in the fact that God gave us the sense of touch
because he loves us.

Many of us from that Sunday school program went on to become teachers. My friend Katie became a third-grade teacher. Two of my grade-school classmates also volunteered in the program and became teachers. A girl two years younger than me also volunteered and became a teacher. In fact, Rebecca and I caught up years later when my mother passed. She came to the wake to tell my father and me how much my mother had influenced her decision to become a teacher. A year after that, I met with Rebecca and her students when I did an author visit at her Catholic school. My mom had no idea while she was running that preschool program, but her ability to convince teenage girls to spend their Sunday mornings volunteering as a Sunday school teacher led to a whole army of teachers. These were our humble beginnings. We worked for no pay, but we received valuable experience. And if we're good educators, our growing and learning hasn't stopped since those humble beginnings.

Starting Your Mission

Teaching is a mission, a special call to do important work. No matter how humble our beginnings, all teachers eventually embark on this mission. This was true for Jesus, too. However, he did get kind of a special shout-out when he began his work.

> In those days Jesus came from Nazareth of Galilee and was baptized by John in the Jordan. And just as he was coming up out of the water, he saw the heavens torn apart and the Spirit descending like a dove on him. And a voice came from heaven, "You are my Son, the Beloved; with you I am well pleased." (Mk 1:9–11)

Wouldn't it be awesome if we could start our teaching careers the way Jesus started his? Imagine if your first day of teaching had been like that. You walked into the classroom with all the students watching you. The principal excitedly announced over the P.A. that you were her esteemed teacher, and she was very pleased with you! All the students sat in awe. Without even taking roll, you were already loved and respected. While this has never happened to any teacher anywhere, the truth is that God is pleased with you already. He's delighted you've answered the call to teach.

Although I was pretty sure God was happy with my decision to become a teacher, I was also worried that my mother was never going to agree with my decision. As late as my junior year of college, she was still trying to deter me. She said things to me like, "It's not too late to change majors. You could become an engineer like your dad and your brother. Female engineers make a lot of money—and there would probably be less stress."

I would reply, "I don't want to be an engineer, Mom. I've spent enough summers doing temp work in offices to know I don't want to sit at a desk in a windowless office all day."

But still she would push. "But you're so good at math and science. You'd make a great engineer."

My dad, on the other hand, didn't try to get me to follow in his footsteps. He had a friend who had taught in public schools for many years. From my dad's perspective, it was a pretty dependable job (if you got tenure at a public school) that came with a fairly dependable pension.

Still, my mother's lack of support stung a bit. Nobody wants to feel like she has disappointed her mother with her career choice.

Despite my mother's arguments, I pushed on, did my student teaching, and landed my first teaching job as a long-term sub at a public high school outside of Milwaukee. When that position ended, I returned to my parents' house and took a job teaching seventh- and eighth-grade English at a Catholic school in Illinois. One day I came home with a set of projects to grade. I plopped down in the living room, where my mom was going through some old magazines.

I laughed as I picked up one of my students' projects. "Mom, look at this." I held out a sheet of paper to her. "I asked the students to draw two versions of an idiom: one that shows what the idiom actually means and one that shows what it would be like if we took the idiom literally." I handed her the drawing. "This one's for the idiom 'It's raining cats and dogs.'"

Mom examined the drawing. On one side, the student had drawn a scene of pouring rain. On the other side, cats and dogs were literally falling from the sky.

I rifled through my papers. One after another I handed her some of the better examples. "Aren't these great?" I asked.

She looked at the papers before her and then smiled at me. "I think your students are really lucky to have you as a teacher." Mom didn't say things like this often. She wasn't one to give praise just for the sake of it. She was never about feeding anyone's ego.

I took the papers back quietly, not knowing what to say next. She might as well have opened the heavens and said, "You are my beloved daughter; with you I am well pleased."

I don't know if you've ever had a similar moment where a family member has told you how proud they are of your decision to become a teacher. But when you are feeling burned out, remember this: You are a beloved son or daughter of God, and whether you teach for one year or forty years, he is well pleased with you.

REFLECTION QUESTIONS

1. Think about a time you felt that you were called to be a teacher. Was it scary, exciting, a mixture of the two? Have your feelings about teaching changed since then?
2. What were your "humble beginnings," and how did God use them to prepare you for teaching?
3. What teachers from your youth inspired you to teach? Was it the really good ones or the not-so-hot ones who got you thinking about what kind of teacher you could be?

TWO

Jesus Had a First Day, Too

Do you remember your very first day of teaching? Not your student teaching, but your actual first day of teaching in your own classroom? I'll be honest. I don't remember mine. It was at a public high school in Wisconsin, where I served an entire school year as a substitute for a teacher who was on disability leave. The students had no idea I was a sub as I was there from day one, and I stayed until the very end of the year.

I remember driving to school. I remember being very nervous. I'm a petite woman, towered over by most high school students, especially the juniors and seniors I was assigned to teach. With my September birthday, I was twenty-one years old for the first three weeks of the school year, and I looked so young for my age that I blended right in with the students. Even when I switched to teaching middle school the next year, I often blended in with the students on field trips, causing museum curators to look over the students and ask, "Where is the teacher?"

While I can remember being nervous on that drive to the first day of teaching high school, I don't recall much else about that particular day. Somehow I made it through, got home, and stayed up late meticulously planning for the next day. This pattern repeated for the entire school year; so much of it is a blur. I remember having a few supportive coworkers and some great students (some whose names and faces are still fresh in my memory), and I remember having some students who seemed to absolutely despise me.

Jesus's First Day of Teaching

As I spent some time reading the gospel passages that depict the beginning of Jesus's public teaching and ministry, it occurred to me that while Jesus was called to begin his public work when he was baptized by John, he didn't get to work immediately. Chapter 3 of Matthew's gospel ends with the baptism of Jesus, and chapter 4 begins with his temptation in the wilderness. Then starting with verse 12, we get a section titled "Jesus Begins His Ministry in Galilee." When I first read that title, I thought, *Oh good, it's like Jesus's first day of teaching!* Yet this is how that section unfolds:

> Now when Jesus heard that John had been arrested, he withdrew to Galilee. He left Nazareth and made his home in Capernaum by the sea, in the territory of Zebulun and Naphtali, so that what had been spoken through the prophet Isaiah might be fulfilled:

"Land of Zebulun, land of Naphtali,
  on the road by the sea, across the Jordan,
    Galilee of the Gentiles—
the people who sat in darkness
  have seen a great light,
and for those who sat in the region and shadow
  of death
  light has dawned."

From that time Jesus began to proclaim,
"Repent, for the kingdom of heaven has come near."
(Mt 4:12–17)

The first thing that struck me about this passage was that Jesus began his teaching right after John was arrested. Yikes. If I had been in Jesus's sandals at that time, and the guy who had announced my coming had just been thrown in the slammer, I would've thought, *Shoot. Things just got real!*

Thankfully, I'm not Jesus. He recognized that this meant it was time to act. I would've been petrified. How could I start preaching about repentance? John was doing the same thing, and they threw him in jail.

I don't know if John's being thrown in jail scared Jesus (I mean, it does say he left Galilee after he heard that), but it is clear that even if he was scared, he didn't let that stop him from beginning his work. Maybe it even spurred him on to get going.

The second thing I noticed was that Jesus turned to the repentance theme right from the start. In both Matthew's and Mark's gospels, Jesus immediately talks about repentance and preparing for the kingdom of God. Did everyone start following Jesus's teaching right away? No. It took time for Jesus's message to work its way into the hearts of his followers, and in the end, many others rejected his message.

What does this mean for us teachers? First, we need not be disheartened if we don't work a miracle on our first day, or in our first week, or even in our first few years of teaching. If people didn't listen to Jesus right from the start, we have no reason to believe that we are going to be any more successful on our first day or first week of any given school year.

At the same time, I think it's helpful to remember that teaching offers us many opportunities to start again, to have "first days." Obviously, the beginning of each school year offers a fresh start, but there are many other times that we can begin again. Turning to a new unit is a time to start fresh. If the last unit didn't go as planned, it doesn't mean this unit can't be better. If the time before Christmas break was crazy and hectic, we can start again with a new seating chart in January. As a middle school teacher, I can even get a fresh start at the beginning of each forty-minute class period. Just because my lesson flopped in period one doesn't mean it will flop in period two. It's a new group of students. They might react differently. I could also change up the lesson plan a bit.

If you find yourself struggling to make it through the school year, figure out a way you can have a fresh start. Can you rearrange your classroom? Can you reorder your daily procedures? Can you try a totally new lesson plan you've never tried before? Can you collaborate with a colleague to do something different? Maybe even partner up with a teacher in a different grade? One of the benefits of being a teacher for many years is getting to reuse old lesson plans, but if those plans are dragging you down, find a way to make tomorrow a new "first day."

And if it flops, that's okay. Another first day is right around the corner. As Anne said to Marilla Cuthbert in *Anne of Green Gables*: "Isn't it nice to think that tomorrow is a new day with no mistakes in it yet?"

Remember your Purpose

The gospels show us that Jesus was clear about his purpose. Right from the first chapter of Mark, Jesus begins healing people, starting with Simon's own mother-in-law.

> As soon as they left the synagogue, they entered the house of Simon and Andrew, with James and John. Now Simon's mother-in-law was in bed with a fever, and they told him about her at once. He came and took her by the hand and lifted her up. Then the fever left her, and she began to serve them. (Mk 1:29–31)

Word travels fast, and soon everyone is bringing people to Jesus to be healed:

> That evening, at sunset, they brought to him all who were sick or possessed with demons. And the whole city was gathered around the door. And he cured many who were sick with various diseases, and cast out many demons; and he would not permit the demons to speak, because they knew him.
>
> In the morning, while it was still very dark, he got up and went out to a deserted place, and there he prayed. And Simon and his companions hunted for him. When they found him, they said to him, "Everyone is searching for you." He answered, "Let us go on to the neighboring towns, so that I may proclaim the message there also; for that is what I came out to do." (Mk 1:32–38)

What I love here is that Jesus makes his purpose very clear. In fact, in the translation I read on retreat, *purpose* is the word used in the passage: "Let us go on to the nearby villages that I may preach there also. For this purpose have I come" (Mk 1:38,

NABRE).[4] I remember putting my small book of the gospels down and looking around at the retreat-center room and pondering this line for a moment. Is preaching my purpose? Is that why God sent me? And what exactly does that mean?

I also recalled a colleague who, when we were faced with a particularly challenging student who had many special emotional needs, said to me, "You know, this isn't what I signed up for. I signed up for teaching, not dealing with all these emotional problems these kids have got." Although I didn't say it to that colleague at that time, I thought, *Wait a minute. Isn't this what we signed up for? We signed up for teaching, and sometimes that involves way more than math or science or reading or social studies or religion.*

As I look back over my career, I think about some of the teaching positions I've held. While none of them were in what might be deemed particularly challenging neighborhoods, on more than one occasion I've had to deal with gang activity. A student at the high school where I first taught tried to start a gang in a town that was half suburban, half rural. One morning while I was watching the news before school while eating my breakfast, video footage of my student being walked out of school in handcuffs flashed on the screen. The newscaster explained that he had been arrested straight out of school the day before. Later that morning, another one of my students filled me in on the details. She was a former gang member from Chicago. Her father had moved her and her sister up to the suburbs of Milwaukee after her best friend died in her arms—shot by a rival gang member. She had laughed at the boy's attempt to start a gang, explaining to me that he was mixing up symbols, signs, and colors from different gangs.

When I switched to teaching at a Catholic school, I thought I had escaped dealing with gang issues, but some of my students were harassed by local gang members on their walks to and from school. Another student got involved with the wrong crowd and was caught with drugs on a school field trip.

A few years later, while employed at a different Catholic school, I spent a couple summers teaching at a public middle school attended by members of two different gangs. I was trained to watch for common gang symbols and spent the summers telling kids to take rubber bands off the bottoms of their jeans because it was a symbol for one of the local gangs.

When I chose teaching as a career, I did not intentionally (or knowingly!) sign up for gang-symbol patrol or suicide watch (my heart aches over the numerous students I've had with suicidal ideations) or being alert to eating disorders or serious illnesses or broken homes or any of the myriad other challenges students face. Like Jesus, my purpose is to teach, but teaching requires recognizing the whole person, as best we can. If you're feeling burned out because you can't reach every kid, remember that Jesus didn't stay and heal every single person either. He chose to move on to other towns to preach. At the same time, he didn't ignore the pain and illnesses he encountered wherever he went. He reached out with compassion.

As you start each school day afresh, remember *your* purpose. You are here to teach with compassion. If you can keep that focus as you start each day, you'll always have a purpose that will keep you coming back to teaching.

It can also help to think of your unique talents and passions as a teacher. While all of us are called to teach with compassion, we each bring something different to the game. It's that something different that can help us find our unique purpose as a teacher.

Maybe you are passionate about reaching English language learners. Maybe you're passionate about helping students see how math is relevant to our everyday lives. Maybe you're really knowledgeable about the ways faith and science intersect. For me, it's all about kids and books. Even though I knew from the beginning of my education courses that I wanted to be an English teacher and not a math, science, or social studies teacher, it still took years before I realized that books for kids were what I was most passionate about. While pursuing my master's degree in language arts instruction, I had to come up with a mini proposal for a research topic. I chose to research and write about grammar instruction because it's something I see so many of our schools falling away from while our students' writing skills seem to get weaker and weaker. However, what I learned during that pseudo–master's thesis is that I did not want to go on to write a dissertation on grammar instruction for my doctoral degree!

The professor who oversaw that project warned me and another classmate not to pursue our doctorates until we had found a topic that we loved so much we were willing to spend years researching it. I took that as a sign not to start my doctorate right away. I did not want to spend years researching grammar instruction, even though it remains to this day a topic I care about deeply. As a result, I didn't choose to pursue my doctorate until after I'd written the manuscripts for my first YA book and my first middle-grade book. By the time my second book was accepted for publication, I had already spent years studying literature for adolescents. I knew I had a topic I could stand to research over the long haul. It was then that I realized that matching up kids with great books was a definite part of my purpose. That is not to say that I ignore the other aspects of being an English teacher. Of course not. However, if you find yourself lacking in passion for your teaching, it might be time to ask yourself what part of this job might ignite that passion again. Jesus was clear about his purpose. It's good for us to be clear about ours, too.

REFLECTION QUESTIONS

1. Think of a way you can create a fresh start on your next day of school.
2. What is something you have learned about teaching since you first began? Does it make you hopeful for how you can continue to grow as a teacher?
3. What do you see as your unique purpose as a teacher?

THREE

Jesus Put the Children First

While I was attending Marquette, the student newspaper would occasionally publish "he said/she said" articles about different topics. A female student would take one side of the argument; a male student would take the other side. In one edition, the topic was whether or not teaching was a worthy career choice. The male writer made fun of people who chose education as a career. I don't remember his exact arguments, but I seem to recall nonsense about our college classes being easy compared to his business classes and about how we'd never make any real money as educators. As you might imagine, I was offended. I didn't choose teaching because I thought the required course-work would be easy. And while I knew that teachers made far less than the average business graduate, I certainly did not need him rubbing my nose in that fact!

Unfortunately, what was even worse was the female writer's response. She was an education major trying to defend our common career choice, but our major seemed to be the only thing we had in common. We had very different ideas about what a career as a teacher would be like. She attempted to defend education majors by writing, "Well, enjoy your office job! I might not make a lot of money in the future, but I'll be the one laughing all summer long and when I get to walk out of work at 3:30 every day."

I didn't have to complete one day of student teaching to come to the conclusion that she wasn't going to last long in the profession. If you signed up for this job for the summers off, I'm the one laughing because I'm betting you've worked more than one summer to make up for your lack of a living wage. And if you signed up to teach because you thought you'd be done working every day at 3:30, then I weep for you because you had no clue what you were getting yourself into.

Let's be honest. Anyone who became a teacher because they thought they would have summers off and would only have to work seven hours a day became a teacher for the wrong reasons. If you find yourself frustrated at putting in fifty-hour weeks, take some time to think about the only reason why anyone should get into teaching at all.

All the Children

You signed up for teaching because you like kids, right? Sure, maybe you picked a certain content area that interests you, especially if you teach high school or middle school. But if you didn't sign up because you like working with kids, then you might want to consider whether this is the reason you are burning out. If you decided to teach because you do like kids, then maybe it's time to reflect and remember that they are the reason you do what you do.

One of my favorite gospel scenes is when Jesus lets the little children come to him. Let's take a look at this scene and imagine Jesus as a teacher gathering the children close to him.

> People were bringing little children to him in order that he might touch them; and the disciples spoke sternly to them. But when Jesus saw this, he was indignant and said to them, "Let the little children come to me; do not stop them; for it is to such as these that the kingdom of God belongs. Truly I tell you, whoever does not receive the kingdom of God as a little child will never enter it." And he took them up in his arms, laid his hands on them, and blessed them. (Mk 10:13–16)

I love how tender Jesus is in this scene. On the one hand, he is indignant that his disciples see the children as being unimportant and want to push them away from him. The disciples even rebuke the parents who are trying to get their children near enough to Jesus so he can touch them. The disciples remind me of those parents in old movies and books who make comments that children should be "seen and not heard," but they go a step further and want to push the kids out of sight, too. In their view, the children should be neither seen nor heard.

Jesus has a completely different view and gets upset with the disciples. Not only does he want the children close to him, but he wants his disciples to be *like* the children. His disciples should not ignore the children, but much more than that, they should even imitate the children in order to enter the kingdom of God.

After rebuking the disciples, Jesus turns tenderly to the children. He draws them close, embraces them, puts his hands on them, and blesses them. Jesus loves kids! Is it any wonder? It seemed to be a surprise to his disciples, but it shouldn't be a surprise to us. Jesus's words and actions are a powerful reminder to us that children are the most important part of our job.

I've been reminded of this gospel passage many times over the years. The first time was during my second year of teaching. It was my first year in the Catholic school system, and I knew that my schedule was going to be more challenging than it had been the previous year. At the public high school where I first taught, my class sizes ranged from five students to twenty-five students, and I had to teach five periods a day and supervise one study hall. At the Catholic school, I had to teach six periods a day and supervise recess twice a week. My class sizes ranged from fifteen to thirty-one.

I gulped when the principal told me I would have thirty-one students in the room at one time. And not just any thirty-one students; I was going to have thirty-one *seventh graders* (read: hormonal and hyperactive) for reading during the very last period of the day in a classroom built seventy years earlier and designed to hold about twenty-five students. The kids were packed in like sardines.

In the days before the school year began, I tried rearranging my desks about four different ways to get them all in there in a way that would foster book discussions. As I sat at my teacher desk and looked over the cramped quarters I would be sharing with my students, the line from Mark's gospel popped into my head: "Let the little children come to me" (Mk 10:14). This was going to have to be my prayer for that school year. I was going to have to want many children close to me just as Jesus did.

Despite our sardine-like conditions, the thirty-two of us survived last-period reading class together. There was not much room for group work, so I had to confine our activities to reading aloud, discussing, and working with an elbow partner, but we did it. We read, we discussed, we laughed. And I can only hope they learned, too.

Two years later, I began teaching at a very small Catholic school. In my fourth year there, we learned the archdiocese had decided to close it. That year, we had only three girls in the eighth grade, one boy in the seventh grade, and eight kids in the sixth grade—a total of twelve kids in middle school. There were four of us who taught grades five through eight. The math teacher taught only in the mornings. The science teacher doubled as the computer teacher and was also the assistant principal. The social studies teacher was also the Spanish teacher. She took the fifth graders as her homeroom. When it came to deciding what to do with grades 6–8, I said I would take them all into my homeroom, and once again, the line from Mark's gospel came to mind: "Let the little children come to me." I could have tried pushing the sixth graders off on the science/computer teacher, but that would have left only four kids in my homeroom— the three eighth-grade girls and the one seventh-grade boy. It seemed wrong to put the one boy with the three girls, so I just swept them all up into my room. I figured it would be more fun for them all to be together than to split up the small amount of work it takes to be a homeroom teacher.

When that school closed, I moved to a school with more typical class sizes, but there have still been times when I've felt a little packed in my classroom that was built in an era long before students were lugging tablets and/or laptops around with them everywhere. Please don't think that I'm saying it's in the children's best interest for us to have oversized class groupings. But I do think it's worth our time to remember that *they* are the reason why we are here. If you're feeling overwhelmed by the number of papers to grade or the demands on your time from your principal or the emails from parents, take a deep breath and remember the words of Jesus. Not only are we to let the children come to us, but we are also called to accept the kingdom of heaven as they would. Focus on them. They are the reason we became teachers, and in the end, it is our relationships with them that will be remembered long after the paper grading is finished.

You're Here for the Tax Collectors

Now you might be thinking, "Sure, Amy, I'm happy to take *all* the children, as long as *all* the children does not include *those* children." You know the ones: the students who need a personal invitation to follow our instructions even after we've repeated them to the class three times, or the ones who roll their eyes at us when they hear our instructions, or the ones who heard our instructions and didn't roll their eyes but just went ahead and did what they wanted to do because none of the rules apply to them anyway. You might be thinking, *Sweet Jesus, I'll take a thousand children, just make all of them really compliant and easy to teach.*

There are only two problems with saying that: (1) no class is perfect. Every class has at least one child that is going to challenge our sanity once in a while, and (2) that's not why God called us to be teachers.

Let's turn to Matthew's gospel to see how Jesus handles someone that other people look down on:

> As Jesus was walking along, he saw a man called Matthew sitting at the tax booth; and he said to him, "Follow me." And he got up and followed him.
>
> And as he sat at dinner in the house, many tax collectors and sinners came and were sitting with him and his disciples. When the Pharisees saw this, they said to his disciples, "Why does your teacher eat

with tax collectors and sinners?" But when he heard
this, he said, "Those who are well have no need of
a physician, but those who are sick. Go and learn
what this means, 'I desire mercy, not sacrifice.' For
I have come to call not the righteous but sinners."
(Mt 9:9–13)

As a tax collector, Matthew was despised. He worked for the
enemy! He took money from his fellow Jews and gave it to the
Roman government. To make matters worse, tax collectors often
took more than they should have because that was how they
earned their living. For this reason, the term "tax collector" was
often associated with and written alongside the term "sinner"
as in this passage. Nobody wanted to hang out with the tax
collectors.

And yet Jesus stops at Matthew's tax booth and calls him
forth. He not only tells Matthew to follow him, but he also dines
with him and other sinners. This baffles the Pharisees to no
end. Why would Jesus associate with such *terrible* people? Jesus
responds simply that they are the reason he has come. He came
to save sinners, not the righteous.

What does this say to us as teachers? Did you become a
teacher just for the well-behaved students? Are you here only to
work with the kids who are already on the "right" track? Maybe
you don't care how book-smart your students are as long as they
all get along, right? Hey, if you can easily put them in partner
work with anyone else in the classroom, that's a good thing! But
what about those kids nobody else likes, the ones who aren't
good at partner work? Or the ones who refuse to work at all and
live off the efforts of their assignment partners?

This passage of Matthew's gospel has challenged me to look
differently at those students who are most likely to add to my
feelings of burnout. Let's be honest, kids who don't get along
with others are exhausting. You're constantly looking for ways

to rearrange your seats and your group work so that you don't have to stick that one kid with the same super-well-behaved kid time and time again. Maybe you've even considered giving up on group work altogether so you don't have to deal with other students complaining that they have so-and-so in their group. Or maybe you've given up on putting your desks in pairs or tables so that no one is forced to sit next to the kid who has no sense of space and leaves books, pencils, and papers in disarray in a wide circle around his desk, almost like marking his territory.

Nonetheless, it is for students just like these that we have become teachers. Which students need us more? The healthy ones or the sick ones? The ones who have already figured out how to get along with others and make friends or the ones who are cluelessly rolling through life not realizing they are their own worst enemy?

But there is more to be gleaned from this passage than just being welcoming to these students in our classrooms. Jesus might be offering us some advice on *how* to deal with them. Notice that Jesus didn't just have dinner with Matthew. He invited Matthew to follow him. In fact, he calls Matthew to be one of his twelve apostles. The tax collector becomes part of the inner circle of Jesus's friends!

How can you make that "tax collector" kid part of *your* inner circle? How can you make the kid that other kids (and quite possibly even other teachers) can't stand feel welcome and a part of your classroom community? Sometimes this might start by just talking with the child on a one-on-one basis. Elementary-school teachers probably have more opportunities for this as they keep the same students in their room for almost the entire school day. They might be able to find times during quiet activities or transition times when they can walk around to students and work with them one-on-one. If you teach middle school or high school, this might be harder, but I've found ways to

engage students before class starts or after it ends. I've been fortunate enough to teach mostly in small schools where I could
catch students in the hallway and ask how their day is going or
whether or not they plan to try out for the next seasonal sport
or the next drama club play. This can help to break down the
wall that students who live on the fringe often put up to protect
themselves from being hurt.

Another common trick many experienced teachers know is
to make the kids who drive you the craziest your special helpers
in class. Put those students to work passing out papers, collect-
ing assignments, organizing your bookshelves, or hanging up
posters. Obviously, some students will be a better fit for this
than others, but if nothing else, it will shake things up. Have
you ever seen *The Calling of St. Matthew* by the Italian painter
Caravaggio? One of the things I love about this painting is the
look on Matthew's face as Jesus points to him, calling him forth
to follow him. Matthew is clearly surprised and more than a
little confused. He even points back at himself as if to say, "Me?
Are you sure?"

If you find yourself burning out because of the "tax collectors" nobody in your school seems to like, think about how you
can turn this story on its head. What can you do to surprise
the tax collector in front of you? How can you shake up the
assumption everyone has fallen into that this kid will never be
anything better?

By Your Students You'll Be Taught

My mom was fond of quoting a line from the musical *The King and I* about how teachers are often taught by their pupils. I don't remember how old I was when I first heard her say it. I don't even think I was a teacher yet, but the line stuck with me—and was reinforced time and time again as I learned different things from my students.

In his early years, Jesus proved that teachers could be taught by their young pupils. Remember what happened when his parents lost sight of him for three days?

> Now every year his parents went to Jerusalem for the festival of the Passover. And when he was twelve years old, they went up as usual for the festival. When the festival was ended and they started to return, the boy Jesus stayed behind in Jerusalem, but his parents did not know it. Assuming that he was in the group of travelers, they went a day's journey. Then they started to look for him among their relatives and friends. When they did not find him, they returned to Jerusalem to search for him. After three days they found him in the temple, sitting among the teachers, listening to them and asking them questions. And all who heard him were amazed at his understanding and his answers. When his parents saw him they were astonished; and his mother said to him, "Child, why have you treated us like this? Look, your father and I have been searching for you in great anxiety." He said to them, "Why were you searching for me? Did you not know that I must be in my Father's house?" But they did not understand

> what he said to them. Then he went down with them
> and came to Nazareth, and was obedient to them.
> His mother treasured all these things in her heart.
> (Lk 2:41–51)

Jesus sat in the middle of the teachers, and what he said amazed them. His questions were enough to make them wonder at his intelligence. Since we know that Jesus is God, it's not overly surprising to us that his teachings would be brilliant and astonishing to those who had no idea who he was. However, notice that Jesus also surprises his own parents, who *did* know who he was! Jesus, however (still a boy at this point), thinks his parents shouldn't have been surprised that he was at his Father's house. After all, they knew exactly who his Father really was! And yet, Mary had to treasure all this in her heart as she grew in understanding of her Son's mission.

Our own students can teach us, too. I'll never forget the student who dropped a very large denomination of currency into our homeroom's Lenten mission can. Granted, I knew that this student came from a wealthy family, and this particular dollar amount might have easily been only a fraction of his birthday money, but it got me thinking, *How much can I put in the mission can?* At that point, I hadn't put in anything yet. His generosity taught me to dig deep and consider how I could contribute.

Over the years I've taught students from many different religious backgrounds, whether it was at a Catholic school or a public school. I've always appreciated what students of other faiths have shared in the classroom. As someone who spent almost her entire education in Catholic schools, I didn't have much of an opportunity to learn about other Christian faiths, much less those outside Christianity. One year I taught an atheist who had a Catholic grandma and had clearly been catechized by her because he seemed to know more about Jesus than many of the cradle Catholics in my room!

My point is to not be afraid to let your students teach you. They may be younger, but they've had different experiences than you've had, and experience is one of the greatest teachers. Let them share their experiences with you.

REFLECTION QUESTIONS

1. Have circumstances kept you from focusing on your students? If you find yourself becoming frustrated with administrators or other teachers or parents who just don't understand why you do what you do, take some time to write a list of all the wonderful moments you've had with your students this past year. Remember that moments like those are the reason you got into teaching.

2. Who is the tax collector in your life right now? What student is getting under your skin? Think of a way you can surprise that student by asking them to do something unexpected, like Jesus asking Matthew to come and follow him.

FOUR

Jesus Set the Stage for Learning

One of the most frustrating things about teaching is that we mature, but our students never do! Think about it. Every new school year, we are older and (hopefully) wiser than we were the year before. Our students, on the other hand, are just as young as they were the previous year because we've gotten a whole new crop of them. Year after year, I get these immature sixth graders, and yet somehow I'm surprised by how little they know! I have to continually remind myself that this is a new group of students, and I have to start from square one.

The sooner we as teachers come to the realization that this situation is not going to change, the happier we will be. Recognize that *you* are reliving kindergarten or fifth grade or freshman year of high school over and over again as you teach the same grade level (or something close to it) year after year. But for your students, this is their first time in this grade or learning this material. That means that every year you must once again set the stage for learning. Try not to see this as a burden. Instead, view it as an opportunity to start something great.

Calming the Waters

Do you ever sit and ponder what Jesus's relationship with his disciples was like? Did he know any of them before he called them? Perhaps he saw some of them around town. Maybe he bought fish from Peter and Andrew. Maybe Matthew had collected taxes from him. Maybe he and his dad Joseph had done carpentry work for the mother of James and John.

If he didn't know any of them ahead of time, how on earth did he convince them to follow him? He must have found some way to develop a relationship with them quickly. Usually, you don't just leave your family and follow a complete stranger. How did Jesus convince them to go with him and to trust him unless he spent time building relationships with them first?

Do we spend time building relationships with our students? To me, there is something sacred about the teacher-student relationship. It's so different from parent-child or even aunt-niece. Without a good student-teacher relationship, learning can be a difficult task. At the very least, our students need to feel they can trust us to teach them what they need to learn. Let's look at a gospel passage about the disciples, Jesus, and the matter of trust:

> On that day, when evening had come, he said to them, "Let us go across to the other side." And leaving the crowd behind, they took him with them in the boat, just as he was. Other boats were with him. A great windstorm arose, and the waves beat into the boat, so that the boat was already being swamped. But he was in the stern, asleep on the cushion; and

> they woke him up and said to him, "Teacher, do you
> not care that we are perishing?" He woke up and
> rebuked the wind, and said to the sea, "Peace! Be
> still!" Then the wind ceased, and there was a dead
> calm. He said to them, "Why are you afraid? Have
> you still no faith?" And they were filled with great
> awe and said to one another, "Who then is this, that
> even the wind and the sea obey him?" (Mk 4:35–41)

Several thoughts occurred to me as I reflected on this passage.
First, we can't just assume that spending time with someone
leads to that person trusting us. This passage occurs in chapter
4 of Mark's gospel. Since his gospel is only sixteen chapters long,
this is already one-quarter of the way through the book. At this
point, the apostles have seen Jesus free a man possessed by a
demonic spirit, cure Simon Peter's mother-in-law (and pretty
much everyone else in Capernaum), cleanse a leper, heal a paralytic, fix a man's withered hand, and preach a bunch of parables.
In fact, as early as chapter 1, verse 28, Mark tells us that Jesus's
fame had spread through the whole of Galilee. Even after wit-
nessing all of that, the apostles still don't trust Jesus to care for
them when a storm rocks their boat. They have to wake him up
and ask him why he doesn't seem to care that they are in trouble.

I don't know about you, but I don't exactly perform miracles
in my classroom. I can't cast out evil spirits or heal a withered
hand. Some days I'm happy to have a Band-Aid in my desk so
I can help a kid cover a paper cut. Yet somehow I have to earn
my students' trust.

Being an authority figure doesn't necessarily bring trust
either. Some of these kids have been terribly hurt by authority
figures. Some have suffered mental, physical, and/or sexual abuse
from those they should have been able to trust. So when the kids
question you, whether it's your knowledge or your assignments
or even just your intentions, try not to take it personally. Their

lack of trust may have nothing to do with you. It's easy for us to think, *I'm the teacher! Of course they should trust me. Of course they should believe I have their best interests at heart.* But if we're honest, we know that these students have probably had teachers who cared more about being off in the summer or leaving work at 3:00 than they did about their students.

One thing I do to build a relationship of trust is make sure I get to know the students and they get to know me. For example, at the start of the school year, I ask the students to write a letter to me introducing themselves. First, I model for them what I want them to do by writing a letter to them introducing myself. I tell them about my family, my education, what I like to do for fun, and even what I like to read (which makes perfect sense as a reading teacher). Then I ask them to write a similar letter back to me.

In recent years, I've added a new twist to this assignment. Since I teach at a school where every student has an iPad, I've turned this into an introductory video assignment. I record a video greeting introducing myself to the students. Then the students create videos introducing themselves to me. An added bonus to the video assignment is that the students record these in their homes, which means they can use props they have close by. Some of them show me artwork they've created, their pile of favorite books or video games, or even their brand-new puppy! By getting to know one another beyond the classroom, we begin to see each other as real people with real lives.

Another thought I had about this passage was that Jesus is great at calming storms, and we need to be great at calming the storms in our students' lives, too. Our students may be young, but they often carry baggage from their home lives into our classrooms. They may be experiencing parents separating or divorcing, the loss of a parent's job, a serious health crisis in a family member, or a parent shipping out to a military deployment. They need our classrooms to be calm seas. If stability is something they can't get at home, we can offer them a few hours of respite from the rocky waves outside our school buildings.

And when the storms enter our schools—through challenges among staff members, belligerent students who argue with every teacher and student, or changes in administration—we need to remember that Jesus can calm our storms, too. Call on him in those moments. When you feel your blood pressure rising, when your patience is wearing thin, offer up this little prayer: *Jesus, calm my storm.*

We don't have to doubt like the apostles did. The Church has more than two thousand years of experience leaning on Jesus to calm its storms. He can calm ours, too.

"Calling" Our Students

When Jesus called people to follow him, he didn't go about earning their trust haphazardly. He knew how to speak their language.

> Once while Jesus was standing beside the lake of Gennesaret, and the crowd was pressing in on him to hear the word of God, he saw two boats there at the shore of the lake; the fishermen had gone out of them and were washing their nets. He got into one of the boats, the one belonging to Simon, and asked him to put out a little way from the shore. Then he sat down and taught the crowds from the boat. When he had finished speaking, he said to Simon, "Put out into the deep water and let down your nets for a catch." Simon answered, "Master, we have worked all night long but have caught nothing. Yet if you say so, I

will let down the nets." When they had done this, they caught so many fish that their nets were beginning to break. So they signaled their partners in the other boat to come and help them. And they came and filled both boats, so that they began to sink. But when Simon Peter saw it, he fell down at Jesus's knees, saying, "Go away from me, Lord, for I am a sinful man!" For he and all who were with him were amazed at the catch of fish that they had taken; and so also were James and John, sons of Zebedee, who were partners with Simon. Then Jesus said to Simon, "Do not be afraid; from now on you will be catching people." When they had brought their boats to shore, they left everything and followed him. (Lk 5:1–11)

When Jesus called his apostles, he did not give a lengthy explanation of what he was asking them to do. He didn't go into a deep theological discussion either. Instead, he used words that they would understand. Since he was talking to fishermen, he explained that they were now going to gather up people just as they had been gathering up fish.

We can do the same when we approach new concepts with our students. It can be frustrating to feel we've explained something clearly only to have our students not grasp the lesson or forget the material about as quickly as they seemed to learn it. This is when it can help to remember that we need to speak in a way that they can relate to.

That's not to say that teachers should be using the latest slang. Although it certainly doesn't hurt to know what expressions they are using, it doesn't mean *we* should be using them, too. What it does mean is that we need to engage our students in ways that are relatable to them. In my doctoral program at Loyola University Chicago, we talked a lot about culturally relevant pedagogy. How do we teach in a way that is relevant to our students' lives? Sometimes this is as simple as figuring out what their background knowledge is and then finding a way to use that knowledge as a hook into the new material. For example, when The Hunger Games and the Divergent series were so popular, it was easy to tap into a quick discussion of how those novels were examples of dystopian fiction before beginning a unit on a classic dystopian novel like *Animal Farm* or *1984*.

As a language arts teacher in a linguistically diverse school in which many students speak other languages at home with their parents and/or grandparents, I have found ways to draw on the linguistic knowledge my students already have. For example, in English we put adjectives in front of nouns. I ask my students who speak Spanish (or another Romance language) to think about how they might say certain phrases like "a blue shirt," in which the adjective would actually go after the noun. Making comparisons and contrasts between the language they speak at home and the language they are learning in school gives the students a chance to literally speak their language in my classroom. I'm teaching the lesson in a way that validates who they are, enriches our class discussion, and improves the chances they are going to remember what they learn. I can't help but wonder if Jesus wasn't thinking along the same lines when he told his disciples they would be fishers of men. He was validating the work they had already done while simultaneously making a connection to the work they were now going to do.

As I reflected on this gospel passage, the last line hit an entirely different chord for me: "When they had brought their boats to shore, they left everything and followed him" (Lk 5:11). The apostles left their families behind when they decided to follow Jesus. Our students don't leave their families behind when they come to us. They bring with them everything that is going on in their home lives and everything they have learned from their parents, siblings, extended family members, even neighbors, friends, and classmates.

While we may not get the undivided attention of our pupils that Jesus received from his apostles, this is not a bad thing. Rather, when we feel we need help in reaching our students, we can approach their parents and ask for their ideas. We can also speak with their past teachers. One of the nicest things about teaching at a Catholic school is that it has the feel of a family. Everyone knows everyone else, and you can easily find out who your student's previous teachers were. If you have students who make you want to bang your head against a wall because nothing you try seems to bring any success, try reaching out to their past teachers. Maybe they have some insight into what is causing the difficulty or an idea of a new approach to try.

REFLECTION QUESTIONS

1. How have you needed to "calm the waters" for your students this past year?
2. What activities have you tried to build relationships of trust with your students, and to strengthen that trust as the year progresses?
3. How can you "speak the language" of your students by making your pedagogy or your curriculum more culturally relevant to them?

FIVE

Jesus Asked for Help

At times, teaching can be an isolating and lonely profession. We spend most of our day in a classroom with young people, which is great because we love kids. However, on more than one occasion, I've had a coworker come to me at lunch or after school and say, "I just need some adult conversation for a little while." Confession: Sometimes that's actually *me* going to a coworker and saying that!

Not only do we spend a lot of time without peer companionship, but unless we have a close partner teacher at our grade level, we're also probably making a lot of curricular and pedagogical choices on our own. This kind of autonomy (especially prevalent in Catholic schools, which aren't weighed down with the bureaucracy that pervades many public schools) can be an attractive part of the profession for those of us who were probably "independent workers" when we were students ourselves. The fact remains, however, that we all need help from our friends now and then. This is especially true when we are suffering from burnout. When our well is dry, it's time to find friends to help us refill it.

The Very First Professional Learning Communities

When we were first studying to be teachers, we had classmates and professors to give us feedback on our lesson plans. Maybe we even had the chance to do a few mock lessons in class and received feedback on both *what* was in our plans and *how* we executed them. Then we moved to our student teaching, and we received advice from our mentor teacher at the school and the supervising professor from the university. Once we finish our degrees, are we done learning in community? If Jesus and his disciples are the examples we hope to follow, then we should probably take the hint that we still need professional learning communities even after our formal education is over.

> [Jesus] went up the mountain and called to him those whom he wanted, and they came to him. And he appointed twelve, whom he also named apostles, to be with him, and to be sent out to proclaim the message, and to have authority to cast out demons. So he appointed the twelve: Simon (to whom he gave the name Peter); James son of Zebedee and John the brother of James (to whom he gave the name Boanerges, that is, Sons of Thunder); and Andrew, and Philip, and Bartholomew, and Matthew, and Thomas, and James son of Alphaeus, and Thaddaeus, and Simon the Cananaean, and Judas Iscariot, who betrayed him. (Mk 3:13–19)

Did Jesus create the first professional learning community when he pulled together his apostles? Maybe, but it makes me smile every time I think of Jesus gathering these twelve guys and taking them up on a mountain to begin forming them as evangelists. What was it like to be part of *that* learning community? Sure, there was that stinker Judas Iscariot (doesn't every group have someone who isn't a team player?), but for the most part, these guys must have had an incredible bond. Do you have that kind of bond with your coworkers?

Given their occasional lack of commitment to the cause (*cough* Peter denying Jesus three times! *cough*) and their competitiveness (I'm looking at you, Sons of Thunder), I'm thinking the disciples probably didn't always know how to proceed with evangelizing. Sure, they had Jesus to help them, but let's not forget there were times when Jesus sent them out two by two, so he wasn't always around to intervene (see Mark 6:7).

Why did Jesus send them out two by two? He knew that they would need each other's support. Nothing about being a new evangelist could've been easy. Can you imagine walking into a strange town all by yourself and declaring that the Messiah had come, but he was not the great warrior and political leader everyone was expecting? The apostles were probably laughed at by some people, ignored by others, and questioned to the point of inquisition by others. By having a partner with them, at least they had someone to help pick them back up again when it got to be too much. They could each try out different tactics for evangelizing and then watch to see how successful their partner's tactic was. If it seemed to work well, they could try adapting that strategy as their own.

Why don't we do this more often as teachers? Why don't we observe each other more in the classroom to see what ideas might be working for others that we could also use? This practice of observing teachers doesn't have to end when we finish our clinical hours. I think this can be especially useful when we're feeling burned out. Trying something new can alleviate the I've-tried-everything-and-nothing-works feeling we sometimes get.

I've worked at schools where administrators have encouraged us to observe our colleagues, and I've witnessed a bit of pushback on this idea. I think there are two reasons for this. First, some teachers worry that other teachers coming to observe them will end up getting them in trouble somehow, as if we are there to spy on one another. If we are genuinely worried that what we are doing in the classroom is not good enough for others to come and watch, either we have really low self-esteem or we need to up our game. Second, I think some teachers have convinced themselves that it is weak to ask for help from another teacher. There is an attitude of "I'm doing everything just fine. I don't need any help from anyone."

Listen, I don't want to toot my own horn, but I'm a fairly smart cookie. I graduated magna cum laude from Marquette, and I have a doctoral degree from Loyola University. I received straight As and a "high pass" (the highest score you can get) on my comprehensive exams. I've also been at this teaching game for about a quarter of a century. Despite all of that, I *still* learn new things about teaching all the time. And I don't just ask veteran teachers for help; I will chase down newbie teachers if I think they've got something useful that will make my job easier or just plain make me a better teacher. This Gen Xer has learned a lot from a few Millennials!

Why do I seek out help from other teachers? Because I truly believe what I tell my students and their parents during parent-teacher conferences: smart kids ask questions and get help when they need it. If you've been teaching more than a year or two, you might very well have said this yourself. Maybe you say it in front of your students, too. Some kids think that only "dumb kids" ask for help. They need us to show them that it's smart to admit when you don't know something or when you want to understand better. And there's *always* room for improvement. We teachers need to take our own advice from time to time.

Hopefully, you teach on a team where you feel comfortable going to others for help. Jesus warned his disciples, "And if a house is divided against itself, that house will not be able to stand" (Mk 3:25). It can be really hard to work at a school where teachers don't get along. If that is the case for you, do your best to develop a good working relationship with at least some of your colleagues. Remember that you all have the children's best interests in mind. None of us entered this profession for the big paycheck. Maybe some of us (like that student in the Marquette newspaper) joined the profession for the summer vacation, but those teachers usually don't last long. Remember also that building these relationships can take time, especially because we spend so much of our day away from our coworkers and with the children.

Outside Sources

What if you were the apostle who was partnered up with Judas? Somebody had to be, right? There Jesus was partnering everyone up and sending them out two by two, and like the weakest kids in gym class, you and Judas Iscariot were the last two left. Jesus turned to you and said, "All right, you two, I'm sending you out together. Go drive out some unclean spirits in the next town over." You might be thinking, *Um, I thought I saw Judas take some cash for himself out of the money bag last week. I'm not sure he doesn't have an unclean spirit himself.*

Sometimes we may be asked to work with teachers who have undesirable qualities. Maybe they are know-it-alls who won't listen to our ideas or resource hogs who won't share with others. If the professional development well within your school is running dry, start looking for ways to refill your bucket outside of school.

One way to do this is to look for professional development activities you can attend either during the school day (if your school lets you take days off for this) or on weekends. Of course, there are those one-day workshops you get flyers for in your teacher mailbox. Does one look interesting? Try asking your principal if there is money for you to go. Your students will survive with a sub for one day. And quite frankly, I've found that just being in a different environment for one or two days has often been enough to recharge my batteries. If you live in a cold climate like I do, this is especially true in February and March when we are all sick of the frigid temps and snow. Not only are you likely to learn at least one or two new things at the workshop, but you'll feel refreshed being around other teachers and having some adult conversation.

Is there a professional conference you can attend? Going out of state might not be in your budget, but check into conferences sponsored by professional education associations. Keep an eye on when the National Catholic Educational Association (NCEA) holds its annual meeting (usually the week after Easter) and make plans to go when it's in your area. Do you belong to any other education associations? Look into the National Council of Teachers of English, National Council of Teachers of Mathematics, National Science Teaching Association, Association for Middle Level Education, International Literacy Association, or the International Society for Technology in Education. There are so many out there. If you're running out of ideas on how to improve your teaching, attending a professional conference could give you inspiration and concrete suggestions.

For cost reasons, it may be hard to attend these conferences often, if at all. If that's the case, reach out to online communities for help. For example, on the first and third Saturday mornings of each month, a group of Catholic schoolteachers meet for a Twitter chat at 9:00 a.m. Eastern. The chat uses the hashtag #CatholicEdChat and lasts for an hour. Each week's conversation has a theme, and the moderator asks questions based on the theme. I stumbled upon this Twitter chat a couple of years ago, and I can say that this is an amazing group of educators who have lots of helpful ideas to offer. Everyone learns from the group's collective knowledge, and ideas can be shared between schools that are sometimes entire states apart. Many have commented that this is the best professional development they get all year—and it's free!

The Nonbelievers

Have you heard of educator Ron Clark or read his book *The Essential 55*? Amazingly, many of his early coworkers actually got mad at him for being successful with his students. They had no luck at getting the students to turn in work, and then in came this young teacher from the South who offered students brownies if they finished all their homework for ten days in a row. Voilà! The kids turned in their homework.[5]

Now I'm not about to tell you to bribe your students with food. Due to the increase in food allergies since Clark wrote his book, many of us teach in schools where bringing in outside food would be tricky if not downright forbidden. I describe this episode because I admire how Clark kept going despite the negative reaction he received from his coworkers for being good at his job!

Perhaps you've been in a similar situation. You are chugging along on your own. Maybe you're getting a little help from outside sources, but the people teaching in the classrooms near you are giving you the evil eye for trying out that new thing you saw

on Pinterest or read about through a link on Twitter or bought
from TeachersPayTeachers.com. In addition to suggesting you
read how Ron Clark dealt with this, I can offer you two biblical
passages for consolation. The first is from early in Mark's gospel:

> They went to Capernaum; and when the sabbath
> came, he entered the synagogue and taught. They
> were astounded at his teaching, for he taught them
> as one having authority, and not as the scribes. Just
> then there was in their synagogue a man with an
> unclean spirit, and he cried out, "What have you to
> do with us, Jesus of Nazareth? Have you come to
> destroy us? I know who you are, the Holy One of
> God." But Jesus rebuked him, saying, "Be silent, and
> come out of him!" And the unclean spirit, convuls-
> ing him and crying with a loud voice, came out of
> him. They were all amazed, and they kept on asking
> one another, "What is this? A new teaching—with
> authority! He commands even the unclean spirits,
> and they obey him." (Mk 1:21–27)

When Jesus began his preaching, people were taken aback.
They didn't quite know what to make of it. They questioned
each other, "What is this?" His "new teaching—with authority"
had them all scratching their heads. Therefore, take heart if your
way of teaching sometimes throws other people for a loop. We
tend not to like change, and when we see someone new come
in or someone trying something new, it may take us a while to
accept that change.

And what if they never accept the way you want to do things?
What if you have Negative Nancy colleagues who have fallen
into the trap of being bitter? Then remember these words that
Jesus spoke in Matthew's gospel:

So have no fear of them; for nothing is covered up that will not be uncovered, and nothing secret that will not become known. What I say to you in the dark, tell in the light; and what you hear whispered, proclaim from the housetops. Do not fear those who kill the body but cannot kill the soul; rather fear him who can destroy both soul and body in hell. Are not two sparrows sold for a penny? Yet not one of them will fall to the ground apart from your Father. And even the hairs of your head are all counted. So do not be afraid; you are of more value than many sparrows.

Everyone therefore who acknowledges me before others, I also will acknowledge before my Father in heaven; but whoever denies me before others, I also will deny before my Father in heaven. (Mt 10:26–33)

You are worth more than sparrows. God has counted all the hairs on your head (even the gray ones Clairol is covering for me). You are loved and acknowledged by him. Rest in that knowledge.

REFLECTION QUESTIONS

1. Is there someone on your faculty that you can go to for help? Or just to lean on after a hard day?
2. What professional development opportunities would you recommend to coworkers? Is there one you've thought of trying that you could check out?
3. Is there something that helps you to remember that you are loved by God? If so, what is it? If not, can you find something?

When was the last time you spent a few moments resting in that love?

SIX

Jesus Knew When (and How Far) to Bend the Rules

Everyone wants to believe they are an expert at teaching. And I don't just mean the teachers and the administrators. I mean, *everyone*. Parents will tell you how you should teach. Politicians and policy makers will tell you how you should teach. Textbook companies and seminar leaders will tell you how you should teach. Business leaders will tell you how you should teach.

To be fair, some of the things they say may very well be valid—at least part of the time. Parents can certainly help us understand their children better, but that doesn't mean they know how to deal with twenty-five or thirty (or even more!) squirrelly bodies sitting in front of us at the same time, much less the unique demands of our content areas. Politicians and policy makers might offer some guidelines that promote equitable education for all, but their overarching policies might miss the mark within our unique realities. Textbook companies and seminar leaders can provide valuable resources and instructional methods, but only you can decide if those resources and methods fit the needs of your student body. And business leaders can help us understand what skills their future employees need, but well, let's face it, that's probably all they should be telling us because education isn't a business.

The truth is, teachers get a lot of advice and have a lot of "rules" to follow. Sometimes this can be a good thing, but that's not always the case. Sometimes you just have to be a bit of a rule bender, which can be a hard thing for many of us. Many teachers (although not all will admit it) enjoyed school as a kid. Sure, some teachers were the ones breaking the rules and acting as the class clown, but some of us were the rule followers. We didn't just follow the rules; we loved them! They gave our lives order and consistency. If you are one of the rule followers, I feel ya! Sometimes, however, you may have to set some of the rules aside in order to reach your students. Sometimes, the message you are teaching is more important than the *way* you are teaching it.

Breaking the Sabbath

Jesus understood this need to bend the rules every now and then. In fact, it caused him a whole lot of trouble with the Pharisees, who were not happy with him breaking Jewish laws.

> One sabbath he was going through the grainfields; and as they made their way his disciples began to pluck heads of grain. The Pharisees said to him, "Look, why are they doing what is not lawful on the sabbath?" And he said to them, "Have you never read

> what David did when he and his companions were
> hungry and in need of food? He entered the house
> of God, when Abiathar was high priest, and ate the
> bread of the Presence, which it is not lawful for any
> but the priests to eat, and he gave some to his com-
> panions." Then he said to them, "The sabbath was
> made for humankind, and not humankind for the
> sabbath; so the Son of Man is lord even of the sab-
> bath." (Mk 2:23–38)

Jesus explained to the Pharisees that rules about the Sabbath
were put in place to benefit humans, not because God required
them for his own good. The third commandment tells us to keep
the Sabbath holy because God knows *we* need to take time for
rest and worship. However, we also need nourishment to keep
our bodies going. Jesus knew his disciples needed food, just
as David's companions did, so he let them get food. He wasn't
concerned about which food. He was concerned about them
getting what they needed.

We have rules in our schools for good reason. We need to
keep things orderly and fair, but fair doesn't always mean everyone gets the exact same thing. Fair means everyone gets what
he or she needs. For example, you might have a rule in your
class that tests are to be finished within a certain time period.
However, you have a student with an IEP or a 504 plan that
allows for extra time on tests. Perhaps she has attention issues
or is dyslexic. You're going to give that student extra time on the
test because it is part of her educational plan; more importantly,
it's in her best interest. However, what if there's another child,
maybe a boy whose grandparent or beloved pet just passed, and
you can see that the student is struggling to hold it together
during the test? You might decide to give that student extra time,
too, or let him take the test a second time. When you do so, you

are giving that child what he needs, even if it means bending your own rules.

Confession time: When I was a young teacher, I had a really hard time with this, and it gave me a lot of stress. I was a rule follower. Rules were good. Students should follow rules. Always. And I still believe classroom rules and school rules help education run smoothly. However, sometimes I lost sight of the bigger picture. I'll never forget what a very rule-following principal said to me in one of my early teaching jobs. I had a student who came down with some kind of medical issue. I can't remember now exactly what it was—pneumonia, chicken pox, something like that. The school year was coming toward a close, and we knew the student would be out for at least a week, maybe even for the rest of the school year.

I walked into the principal's office and asked what I should do with the work she was going to miss. Should I send it home? Should I hang on to it and have her make it all up when (and if) she came back to school?

To help you appreciate this story, I need to describe this principal a bit. First of all, I loved her. She was a stickler about rules just like me. In fact, the teachers had a dress code that required us to wear stockings (remember nylons, ladies?). I would buy knee-high nylons and wear lots of long skirts so that I was technically following the rules without wearing full-length hose. One of my coworkers went bare-legged in the warmer weather and caught a lot of flak from our principal. That's how much of a rule follower this principal was.

So imagine my surprise when I asked the principal if I should send home the sick girl's missing work and she looked up at me from behind her desk and said, "No, you'll just excuse her from those assignments."

"What?" I sank into the chair opposite her desk. "She just gets to skip the assignments altogether?"

"Yes." She nodded at me. "It's almost the end of the school year. You have enough assignments to give her a grade for the quarter."

"You want me to leave some spots in my grade book *blank* for her?" (For any of my public school friends who might be reading this, let me tell you about one of the joys of teaching at a Catholic school. You *rarely* have blank spots in your grade book. Kids turn in the assignments. *All* the kids. *All* the assignments. Yes, some might be late, but almost all of them get turned in eventually. You rarely have blank spots in your grade book.)

It took a while for me to accept that this basic rule of "all kids do all the assignments" was being broken in this Catholic school. However, as I look back on that decision now, I get it. Whatever health issues the family was dealing with in that last week or two of school were more important than the last couple of assignments of the school year.

I bring this up because a rigid mentality of rule following sometimes causes us a great deal of stress. We have to look at the bigger picture just as Jesus did. If you find yourself getting preoccupied with rule following to the point that it is stressing you out, stop and ask yourself, "In the end, what's best for the student?"

This became abundantly clear during the coronavirus pandemic of 2020. In March of that year, schools everywhere went to remote learning. Teachers scrambled to become adept at eLearning. Students were asked to adapt to new ways of being students. Parents nearly pulled their hair out trying to figure out how to facilitate learning at home. Various online chats questioned what would happen to the students. How much learning would they lose? How far behind would our students fall?

Then I saw an Instagram post by fellow Ave Maria Press author Katie Prejean McGrady, in which she discussed being a student during Hurricane Katrina. Students in parts of

Louisiana lost nearly a year's worth of schooling that year, and yet here she was a grown adult with a successful career, a husband, a daughter, and another child on the way. In other words, whatever education was lost during that time was made up in other ways and at other times.

I tried to keep that in mind while planning my eLearning during the stay-at-home orders. I knew that some of my students would likely be dealing with sick family members, parents who found themselves without jobs suddenly, anxiety about the future for themselves and their families, isolation and loneliness without their friends from school, and homes filled with chaos, confusion, and crisis. I could have chosen to drive myself crazy trying to get through all of the curriculum I normally would have. Instead, I decided to focus on the most important things I thought my students needed to know going forward, and to let go of all the "shoulds" I had about how the school year was supposed to end. What did my students need the most from me, and how could I best help them during this extremely difficult time?

That's the same thing Jesus did with his disciples. What did they need from him on that day they picked grain? Did they need to observe the law about resting from work, or did they need to eat? He chose eating. Since he's Jesus, I'm going to go out on a limb here and say he made the right decision.

Here's another example of Jesus bending the rules he would ordinarily have followed in order to serve people:

> After this there was a festival of the Jews, and Jesus went up to Jerusalem.
>
> Now in Jerusalem by the Sheep Gate there is a pool, called in Hebrew Beth-zatha, which has five porticoes. In these lay many invalids—blind, lame, and paralyzed. One man was there who had been ill for thirty-eight years. When Jesus saw him lying there and knew that he had been there a long time,

he said to him, "Do you want to be made well?" The
sick man answered him, "Sir, I have no one to put me
into the pool when the water is stirred up; and while I
am making my way, someone else steps down ahead
of me." Jesus said to him, "Stand up, take your mat
and walk." At once the man was made well, and he
took up his mat and began to walk.

Now that day was a sabbath. So the Jews said
to the man who had been cured, "It is the sabbath;
it is not lawful for you to carry your mat." But he
answered them, "The man who made me well said
to me, 'Take up your mat and walk.'" They asked
him, "Who is the man who said to you, 'Take it up
and walk'?" Now the man who had been healed did
not know who it was, for Jesus had disappeared in
the crowd that was there. Later Jesus found him in
the temple and said to him, "See, you have been
made well! Do not sin any more, so that nothing
worse happens to you." The man went away and
told the Jews that it was Jesus who had made him
well. Therefore the Jews started persecuting Jesus,
because he was doing such things on the sabbath.
But Jesus answered them, "My Father is still working, and I also am working." For this reason the Jews
were seeking all the more to kill him, because he was
not only breaking the sabbath, but was also calling
God his own Father, thereby making himself equal
to God. (Jn 5:1–18)

In reflecting on this passage, I am first struck by the fact that
the religious leaders tell this man that he is being unlawful for
carrying his mat. Do they even know this man's backstory? Do
they have any idea what a miracle it is for him to be *capable* of
walking and carrying his own mat?

How often does something like this happen to our own students? *You* know that a certain child has been reluctant to read all year, but then that same child suddenly discovers graphic novels and is so entranced he carries around a small stack at all times so he can read a few more pages whenever he has a spare moment. Then another teacher comes along, sees him reading the graphic novels, and chides him for spending his time on "comic books." When the kid complains to you that Teacher X took all the graphic novels from him, you want to find Teacher X and scream, "Do you have any idea what a miracle it is that that kid is reading at all? Redirect the student to his assignment, as necessary, but please don't pull from him the only reading I've seen him do all year!"

What lesson is Jesus teaching us through the Jewish leaders' reaction to the man carrying his mat? Sometimes we need to learn a student's backstory before we make a judgment call. When a student fails to follow a rule, we have to find out why. What motivated the student to do this? Get at the heart of the issue before letting your blood boil. Maybe there's no need to get upset about the rule breaking at all. Think about it. The religious leaders in this passage were upset when they should have been rejoicing. Jesus had just healed the man! What they saw as rule breaking was actually a miracle.

The religious leaders in this story persecuted Jesus because he was doing work on the Sabbath. Sometimes something similar may happen to us. We might let a student "get away" with something because we know that what the student is doing is actually a sign of moving in the right direction. Just as Jesus was attacked by others for encouraging the man to carry his mat on the Sabbath, so too might we be criticized by other teachers for allowing our students to do something they wouldn't let the student do. If you're caught in one of those moments where a colleague is chiding you, take comfort in knowing that Jesus understands your pain. Not everyone agreed with his methods either.

All this is to say that sometimes we have to set aside our "shoulds." We need not worry about what we should be doing according to all the educational rules we've been given 100 percent of the time. Instead, we should focus on what works for our students in both the moment and the long term.

Slashing the Red Tape

One aspect of teaching that I struggle with is the pervasive bureaucracy. Sometimes trying to do what works for your students means slashing through some red tape. At a Catholic school, there is often less of this than at a public school. Teachers in Catholic schools tend to be a bit more autonomous because there are fewer layers of administrators micromanaging them than there are in public schools. Administrators in Catholic schools also tend to have greater freedom than their public school counterparts since they also have fewer higher-ups to report to and are not tied as tightly to state education laws. However, that doesn't mean that a teacher in a Catholic school won't have to work her way through some red tape to get done what her students need her to do.

I am reminded of this need to get creative in solving problems when I reflect on the burial of Jesus. He was crucified by the Romans, who would've been happy to leave his body on the Cross and let the vultures take care of it. At the time of his Crucifixion, Jesus was abandoned by many of his disciples, who fled in fear. John, the beloved disciple, was the only apostle there, and he was joined by a handful of women. When Jesus died, it was just prior to the Sabbath so no one could do the work required to prepare his body properly for burial. What on earth was to be done? All four evangelists recount the burial of Jesus in a similar fashion. Here is John's account:

> After these things, Joseph of Arimathea, who was a
> disciple of Jesus, though a secret one because of his
> fear of the Jews, asked Pilate to let him take away the
> body of Jesus. Pilate gave him permission; so he came
> and removed his body. Nicodemus, who had at first
> come to Jesus by night, also came, bringing a mix-
> ture of myrrh and aloes, weighing about a hundred
> pounds. They took the body of Jesus and wrapped
> it with the spices in linen cloths, according to the
> burial custom of the Jews. Now there was a garden
> in the place where he was crucified, and in the gar-
> den there was a new tomb in which no one had ever
> been laid. And so, because it was the Jewish day of
> Preparation, and the tomb was nearby, they laid Jesus
> there. (Jn 19:38–42)

The first thing I'm struck by in this passage is that the two men who came forward to care for his body had followed Jesus secretly. Joseph of Arimathea was a secret follower of Jesus because he feared repercussions from other religious leaders. Both Mark's and Luke's accounts of this story explain that Joseph of Arimathea was a member of the council, meaning that he was part of the Sanhedrin, the Jewish high court that had ordered Jesus's arrest, trial, and death (see Mark 15:43; Luke 23:50). Joseph of Arimathea certainly wouldn't have garnered a great deal of support from his fellow members of the Sanhedrin in trying to ensure that Jesus received a proper burial.

Nicodemus, another member of the Sanhedrin, was also a Pharisee, a group of Jews who were deeply devoted to upholding the law. We see Nicodemus first in chapter 3 of John's gospel when he meets with Jesus at night. Why did Nicodemus meet Jesus after dark? As a Pharisee, he was afraid of how the others would respond if they saw him meeting with Jesus, who was already identified as a rule breaker by the Pharisees.

So here we have two rich, high-standing (from a social hierarchy perspective) men who came forward to break the rules in order to give Jesus a proper burial. At the time, Romans allowed the Jews to take the bodies of Jewish criminals off crosses and bury them in a mass grave. However, Joseph of Arimathea went directly to Pilate and asked for Jesus's body because he wanted to give Jesus a proper burial, not a burial for a criminal. He slashed through the red tape. On top of that, Nicodemus brought one hundred pounds of myrrh and aloes to anoint Jesus's body. One hundred pounds? Have you ever stopped to think about that detail? How did Nicodemus even carry one hundred pounds of spices to the burial spot? Did he use a cart? Was someone else there to help him? He wasn't breaking through red tape in any small way. He seems to have come at it with a go-big-or-go-home attitude.

Then Joseph of Arimathea gave up his own new tomb so that he and Nicodemus had a place to put Jesus's body. According to John, these two men wrapped his body in spices and linen. This was a job that women usually took care of, but they didn't care. They just did it. They bent the rules. Why? Because they loved Jesus! They wanted to care for him as best they could.

Sometimes we have to be like that in our teaching jobs, too. We have to ignore what our peers among the Pharisees and the Sanhedrin tell us we "should" do. We may have to go right to the top (to the Pilates in our lives), ask what others might think is unthinkable, and then argue our case in such a way that they give in. Just as Joseph of Arimathea and Nicodemus put their love for Jesus above their self-interest and their love of Jewish law and custom, so must we adjust our actions to match our priorities.

I can think of two times I was really glad I set aside the "this is what we should do" attitude at the Catholic school where I was teaching. By the way, often this attitude stems from a "this is what we've always done, so we're gonna keep doing it this way" mentality. However, doing something a certain way for years doesn't mean it's still the best thing for students. Keep in mind what we discussed in chapter 3. You're here for the students, so let that guide you more than history or custom. We just need to make sure our motivation is pure. We don't want to turn into nonconformists who break or bend the rules simply because we feel like it. If we're going to bend the rules, let's do it for the students, not ourselves.

The first time I bucked the system a bit was when a group of eighth graders asked me if they could have a real yearbook. This was at St. Philip the Apostle School, the tiny Catholic school where I had the pleasure of teaching for the last four years its doors were open. I had been the yearbook moderator at my previous Catholic school, so I knew how a school yearbook was published. The more yearbooks you bought from the publisher, the cheaper the books were. With such a small student body (St. Philip's had about one hundred students, the bulk of them preschoolers who weren't too interested in purchasing yearbooks), I knew the cost per yearbook would be astronomical.

Nonetheless, I empathized with these kids. The Catholic grade school I had attended didn't have a traditional all-school yearbook either. Instead, only the eighth graders received a yearbook that was really just a set of mimeographed papers with a plastic spiral binding. Despite its simplicity, it was a cherished part of the eighth-grade rite of passage at my alma mater.

Armed with that image in mind, I headed into the principal's office. Yes, the same principal who was the rule follower. I might not have had all the answers in my early years of teaching, but I did have some pretty bold courage when I felt something was in the best interest of the kids. I begged her to help me think of a way we could offer a yearbook to the student body. We discussed the financial challenges. I volunteered to head up a yearbook committee (no stipend involved, thank you), and I shared the simple, mimeographed yearbook I'd had as an eighth grader. Suddenly, the principal's face lit up.

"You know," she said slowly, "we have a family in the school that owns a printing business. Maybe we could get them to run off the pages and bind them for us."

Voilà! The school got a yearbook, and all because I wasn't going to let some red tape from expensive yearbook publishers or a this-is-how-we've-always-done-it (or *not* done it!) mentality stop me.

A similar situation occurred not too long after that. The students wanted a student council, a *real* student council. Every year, I took the seventh and eighth graders (mind you, this ranged from four to nine kids in the four years I was there) to a leadership day held at a local Catholic high school. This leadership day, which was run by the student council members at the high school, was designed to train the junior high student council members from the feeder schools. Every year we came back from the leadership day, we'd have a conversation like this:

"Ms. Cattapan, it was *sooo* embarrassing."

"What was?"

"Talking with the kids from other schools."

"Why?"

"They kept asking us which of us was the president and the vice-president and the secretary, and we don't have that."

"Well, yeah, we're a small school. You all do the work of a student council together. We don't have elections for actual positions."

"Could we have real elections for real positions?"

"You all want to run against each other?"

"Yes!"

You know what happened next, right? I marched myself back into the principal's office. More discussing. More brainstorming. Voilà! We had our first student council election the next year.

Why do I bring all this up? I think what can frustrate us the most in teaching is feeling like we can't help our students. Admittedly, some things are outside of our control. I can't control what happens when my students go home. I can't control whether they are well fed or well supervised or go to bed at a good time. I can, however, look at what is within my control. I can bust through the red tape and the outdated mentalities and try something new. Is it going to work all the time? No. But when it does work, savor the victories. Know that either way, you've fought the good fight for your students.

Tradition!

As Catholics, we are known for a Church that is built on scripture and tradition. Not really a big surprise when you think of how important both scripture and tradition are within our Jewish roots. (As a fan of musicals, I recall the song "Tradition" from *Fiddler on the Roof*.) So I feel it necessary at this point to say that I'm not arguing against tradition, especially not Tradition with a capital T. However, Jesus himself made a point that we should not be slaves to human traditions.

> Now when the Pharisees and some of the scribes who had come from Jerusalem gathered around him, they noticed that some of his disciples were eating with defiled hands, that is, without washing them. (For the Pharisees, and all the Jews, do not eat unless they

thoroughly wash their hands, thus observing the tradition of the elders; and they do not eat anything from the market unless they wash it; and there are also many other traditions that they observe, the washing of cups, pots, and bronze kettles.) So the Pharisees and the scribes asked him, "Why do your disciples not live according to the tradition of the elders, but eat with defiled hands?" He said to them, "Isaiah prophesied rightly about you hypocrites, as it is written,

> 'This people honors me with their lips,
> > but their hearts are far from me;
> in vain do they worship me,
> > teaching human precepts as doctrines.'

You abandon the commandment of God and hold to human tradition."

Then he said to them, "You have a fine way of rejecting the commandment of God in order to keep your tradition! For Moses said, 'Honor your father and your mother'; and, 'Whoever speaks evil of father or mother must surely die.' But you say that if anyone tells father or mother, 'Whatever support you might have had from me is Corban' (that is, an offering to God)—then you no longer permit doing anything for a father or mother, thus making void the word of God through your tradition that you have handed on. And you do many things like this." Then he called the crowd again and said to them, "Listen to me, all of you, and understand: there is nothing outside a person that by going in can defile, but the things that come out are what defile." (Mk 7:1–15)

Jesus makes a clear distinction here between human traditions and God's commandments. The Pharisees and the scribes in this story confused the two. They held their human precepts at the same level as God's laws. When you are agonizing over whether to go against a tradition at your school or conventional ideas about education in general, consider whether that tradition or those ideas align with God's commandments and the way Jesus would teach.

Eliminating the Negative

Even if we have garnered a great deal of support for whatever changes we'd like to implement, I have found that no matter how fabulous the school where I work, no matter how wonderful my coworkers or my students or their families or my administrators, there is bound to be some negativity in there somewhere. Perhaps it's that Negative Nancy of a colleague or someone in a leadership position that has decided to go off the deep end when it comes to workplace expectations. Perhaps we've even let negativity creep into our own hearts. How are we to respond? If someone's negativity is keeping us from doing our best for the students, remember that Jesus has some pretty strong words for that person:

> If any of you put a stumbling block before one of these little ones who believe in me, it would be better for you if a great millstone were hung around your neck and you were thrown into the sea. If your hand causes you to stumble, cut it off; it is better for you to enter life maimed than to have two hands and to go to hell, to the unquenchable fire. And if your foot causes you to stumble, cut it off; it is better for you to enter life lame than to have two feet and to be thrown

> into hell. And if your eye causes you to stumble, tear
> it out; it is better for you to enter the kingdom of God
> with one eye than to have two eyes and to be thrown
> into hell, where their worm never dies, and the fire
> is never quenched. (Mk 9:42–48)

Ouch! Jesus isn't messing around when it comes to people messing with children. This passage comes shortly after Jesus placed a child in the midst of his disciples and told them, "Whoever welcomes one such child in my name welcomes me, and whoever welcomes me welcomes not me but the one who sent me" (Mk 9:37).

What are the stumbling blocks getting in the way of your students' education? Are you putting them there, or is someone else? If it's you, root out the cause and cut it out of your life. If it's someone else, consider what you can do to improve the situation. We might not be able to ignore the coworker with the negative attitude, but we can counter their negativity with our own positive attitude. We can also make the conscious decision to not let that negativity enter our own hearts.

This can be super hard, and I think it's one of the ways we teachers end up sabotaging each other. I saw it as early as my student-teaching days. There are teachers out there who have been in the game so long they've become cynical and bitter. I can't say I entirely blame them. I've seen cynicism creep into my own attitude from time to time. It's hard when we have such high hopes about what our teaching career is going to be like. As I've mentioned, I grew into my decision to become a teacher when movies like *Dead Poets Society, Stand and Deliver,* and *Dangerous Minds* were making it look like every teacher had the possibility to create life-altering moments for all of their students—if only we worked hard enough to do it!

My friends, we do create life-altering moments for our students. It just doesn't happen like it does in the movies. And, I'm sorry to say, it doesn't happen for every student. There are things beyond our control, and that's probably the scariest and the most agonizing part of teaching. We care so deeply for our students that there are moments when we wish we could protect them like any good parent would do.

So what are we to do when this lack of control wears us down and bitter cynicism creeps into our thoughts? We need to do what Jesus told us. We need to pluck out that negativity like it's an eyeball causing us to sin. We need to cut off our cynicism like it's a foot causing us to stumble.

Ignore the coworker (as best you can) who is bringing you down into Negative Nancy world. Counter her cynicism by choosing to find the bright spots in your day. Look for the successes. You *are* changing lives. It can be hard to see because often the change is slow, and it may not even be apparent until years later, but that doesn't mean it isn't happening. You've got to look for the positives; otherwise, you might as well have a great millstone hung around your neck and get thrown into the sea, and who wants that?

REFLECTION QUESTIONS

1. Have you ever put rule following before the best interests of your students? Looking back on it now, would you change what you did?
2. Have you ever uncovered the reason why a student is misbehaving and been surprised by the motivation behind that student's behavior?

3. Have you heard the saying "We've always done it this way" at your school and wondered if that was really in the best interest of the students? How can you combat this mentality?

4. Can you think of ways to counteract the negative and bitter attitudes that can creep into our school communities?

SEVEN

Jesus Knew the Power of a Good Story

This is a chapter I could spend way too much time on. I love a good story. Doesn't matter if it's fiction or nonfiction, just tell me a good one. Don't know one yourself? I'll tell *you* one. Why am I so obsessed with stories? I'm convinced it's in our DNA. God created us to love stories, and we can use them to reinvigorate our teaching.

I love stories so much that I wrote a whole dissertation on how fictitious stories can create empathy for immigrants in middle-grade readers and conducted qualitative research to prove my point. Stories are powerful! They inspire us. They change our perspectives. They help us to heal. If you're feeling a little broken as a teacher right now, I hope my stories and the stories from the gospels we are reflecting on are helping you to heal a bit. Maybe even change your perspective.

The Power of the Parable

Jesus knew the power of story. He used many parables when he preached because he knew that they could be effective teaching tools. In fact, if you look across the three synoptic gospels (Matthew, Mark, and Luke), Jesus used thirty-seven different parables. That's how much Jesus valued stories to help him get his point across.

Sometimes those parables are quite clear. Even young children can grasp the main message of the parable of the good Samaritan. Sure, we can uncover extra layers of meaning in the story as we deepen our understanding of the history between the Jews and the Samaritans; however, the idea of being kind to others, even strangers, is clear right away.

Other parables are harder and require some explanation. Take, for example, the parable of the sower:

> When a great crowd gathered and people from town after town came to him, he said in a parable: "A sower went out to sow his seed; and as he sowed, some fell on the path and was trampled on, and the birds of the air ate it up. Some fell on the rock; and as it grew up, it withered for lack of moisture. Some fell among thorns, and the thorns grew with it and choked it. Some fell into good soil, and when it grew, it produced a hundredfold." As he said this, he called out, "Let anyone with ears to hear listen!" (Lk 8:4–8)

I'm sure this parable made no sense to me when I heard it as a child. First of all, I had no background knowledge in what a "sower" was (is that what you call someone who works a sewing machine?), and I didn't understand much about plant growth. Jesus's followers would have been more familiar with farming than I was as a child (which reminds us of the importance of culturally relevant pedagogy). But even with that cultural relevance for them, they still needed this parable explained to them, too.

> Now the parable is this: The seed is the word of God. The ones on the path are those who have heard; then the devil comes and takes away the word from their hearts, so that they may not believe and be saved. The ones on the rock are those who, when they hear the word, receive it with joy. But these have no root; they believe only for a while and in a time of testing fall away. As for what fell among the thorns, these are the ones who hear; but as they go on their way, they are choked by the cares and riches and pleasures of life, and their fruit does not mature. But as for that in the good soil, these are the ones who, when they hear the word, hold it fast in an honest and good heart, and bear fruit with patient endurance. (Lk 8:11–15)

Jesus had to break this parable down step-by-step for his followers. He explained the symbolic circumstances for the seed on the path, on the rocks, among the thorns, and in the good soil. This is good for us to keep in mind as teachers. Sometimes I think I've explained something so clearly to my students, and then see them looking at me as if I had ten heads. Or else they nod along like they get it, but when I check on their progress later, their work makes it look like they weren't listening at all!

To make matters worse, think of how many times we teachers explain the same thing over and over again. You explain it to the class, and then one child needs it re-explained, and then five minutes later, you're explaining it all over again to another child who didn't pay attention when you gave the instructions to the whole class nor when you re-explained to the other student. If you teach the same subject across multiple classes, even more repetition piles on. By the time you get to the last period of the day, you may have repeated the same instructions eighteen times.

In addition, there's an extra layer of "repeat instruction frustration" that weighs on us, as I mentioned earlier. Not only do we repeat the same instructions within the class period and to multiple class periods on the same day, but we also repeat many of the same instructions year after year after year. When you find yourself feeling frustrated over repeating material, take a deep breath and ask the Lord to grant you patience. And remember that even if it's old news to you, it's new news to your students!

It's helpful to think of all this repetition as part of the scaffolding we do as teachers. You might have explained something very clearly, and 80 percent of your students might be ready to take off running with the brilliant explanation or instruction you gave. However, that doesn't mean there isn't a percentage of the class that needs an extra little step to get to where the rest of the class is. When Jesus shared the parable of the sower, there were probably some in the crowd that understood parts of what he was trying to convey, but struggled with other parts. Maybe they understood the symbolism behind the seeds on the rocky path, but missed the symbolism behind the thorns. Some of our students are going to need more scaffolding, or just different scaffolding, than others.

I was reminded of this need for scaffolding and alternative explanations while attending a teacher workshop at the Chicago Shakespeare Theater. This beautiful theater company offers an annual workshop for teachers where scholars and experts help us learn how to teach Shakespeare to our students. A few years ago, one of the visiting scholars was leading us through a monologue and pointed out something I had never noticed before.

As you may know, Shakespeare wrote for a diverse audience. The peasants stood in the area reserved for the "groundlings." These were the cheap seats, so to speak, although there weren't actually seats at all. You had to stand in the center of the Globe Theatre. If you wanted to sit in one of the seats along the rim of this circular theater, you had to pay more. If you were really wealthy, you sat on a cushion on the highest seats (farthest away from the groundlings). The audience often included very well educated members of society who expected flowery language, complex symbolism, and references to classical literature. However, other members of the audience did not have a classical education and might not understand references to Greek and Roman mythology.

Therefore, some long, flowery monologues in Shakespeare's plays had two parts. The largest part (the beginning) had all the artistic sophistication a well-educated listener could hope for. The last few lines were usually a summary of what had been said at the beginning of the monologue, but in much simpler language. For example, in *The Taming of the Shrew*, the servant Tranio goes into a sixteen-line speech in which he refers to the ancient Greek philosopher Aristotle as well as the Roman poet Ovid. At the end, however, he sums up the whole point of his elaborate speech in one line: "In brief, sir, study what you most affect." [6] In other words, he spent fifteen lines waxing poetic, and then sums up by saying, "In other words, sir, just study whatever you like."

That's what Jesus did with some of his parables. They were beautiful and rich with symbolism, but his followers needed simple explanations sometimes. Don't get discouraged if you have to do the same for your students, especially when introducing something very new to them. I certainly didn't understand everything about Shakespeare the first time I read his plays, and I'm still growing in my understanding of scripture. When you explain something, you're not "dumbing things down." You're building your students up.

Choose Your Parables Wisely

If stories are powerful, then it also matters which stories we choose to share. If you're a reading teacher, think about the stories you assign to your students. Are they worth reading year after year after year? Are there other picture books, novels, or nonfiction works that might have a greater impact on your students? Even if a novel is a good one, you may lose your enthusiasm for it over the years. Perhaps it's time to shake up your routine and try something different.

Teachers of other content areas need to think about the stories they are sharing, too. History teachers have more potential material than they can possibly cover. Consider which episodes of history you spend the most time on. Are those really the most essential? Sure, you need to cover the Civil War if you're teaching American history. But it's worth considering whether you are focusing on the aspects of that segment of our history that will most benefit our students in a country that is still ravaged by racism and discrimination. At the moment, I'm thinking about how few people of my generation were taught about Juneteenth, the date commemorating when the enslaved people in Texas learned about the Emancipation Proclamation, two years after they had officially been freed. While I remember my high school teacher telling us that it took years to get the news of freedom to all those who had been enslaved, I hadn't heard of Juneteenth as the date to commemorate this until I was an adult.

If you teach science, which scientists are you including? Consider ways you can incorporate the stories of lesser-known scientists whose work was groundbreaking. How many female scientists come up in your curriculum? How many scientists of color? Thanks to the movie *Hidden Figures*, we are starting to learn more about women of color in STEM fields. But we can also share about the many influential scientists from the past (and present!) who are priests, monks, and religious sisters. Do your students know that one of the first two people to earn a doctorate in computer science was a nun by the name of Sr. Mary Kenneth Keller, who advocated for the involvement of women in computer-based fields? Are you telling the "story" of how our Catholic faith goes hand in hand with science? This information has the potential to dispel the modern myth that faith and science are opposed.

Even in math class, consider the stories in your word problems. What hidden curriculum might be wrapped in your story problems? The term "hidden curriculum" has been used to refer to ways the dominant culture keeps marginalized groups oppressed, but what if we flipped that idea around? We could use math word problems to infuse our lessons with good values, a respect for people of other cultures, and as a springboard for discussing not just math, but how math impacts our world.

I don't know about you, but this kind of stuff reinvigorates my teaching. Sure, we will always have the same basic learning standards to uphold. Whether we're following the Common Core Standards or not, I'm sure I'll be talking about things like linking verbs and similes until the day I retire from teaching. But what if, when I'm writing example sentences with linking verbs, I use that opportunity to share information about an important person from history my students might not be learning about in social studies or science or math?

While those of you who teach other content areas ruminate on those ideas, I'm going to circle back to the reading teachers. I wrote an entire dissertation on the value of using culturally relevant young adult literature in the classroom, and while I promise

I won't repeat everything from that work here, I will share the most important part of what I took away from that experience.

At the heart of my dissertation is the idea that our students respond strongly to literature that they find relevant. Sometimes that means the character in the book is from the same culture as the student. That's what people normally think of when they think of literature that is culturally relevant. However, as I learned in my research, cultural relevance can have many aspects. Students might relate to the main characters because of age, time period, gender, or setting. It can even be—as my research proved—experiential relevance, in which the students recognize the character encountering something that resonates with their own experiences, such as having to care for a younger sibling, moving to a new school, or being forced to learn a new language.

One aspect of cultural relevance that I've read about but rarely heard discussed in Catholic schools is that of religion! How many stories with Catholic characters do your students read? Maybe you're shrugging your shoulders right now and thinking, "Are there even good novels with Catholic characters out there?" Well, as someone who likes to think she wrote a couple of them, I'd have to say, "Yes!" And I'm not the only one who has done so. The problem is that you probably haven't heard of any of them. Let's face it: Catholic novels aren't likely to show up in your local school book fair that's run by a secular company. Even if a Catholic publisher runs the book fair at your school, they will probably carry only a few novels.

Why is that? First of all, a book fair run by an individual publisher (versus one run by a general bookseller) is going to want to sell the books they publish more than books sold by other publishers. Second, fiction has gotten a bad rap. People tend to think nonfiction is more educational than fiction. And yet, the research I did for my dissertation proves the exact opposite. Students were studying immigration in social studies as well as reading immigration novels in reading class as part of a cross-curricular unit. Time after time in my interviews with the students, they repeated that they had gotten "more information" from reading the novel than they had from studying the topic in social studies. Most interestingly, these comments came from students who were children of immigrants and whose parents had shared with them their own immigration stories. In the conclusion of my dissertation, I argued that there is something about the way that novelists write (their use of sensory details, their figurative language, their mastery of first-person narrators or deep point-of-view third-person narrators) that makes history come to life in a way that facts shared in a history textbook do not.

So what should you do if you want to add some culturally relevant Catholic fiction into your curriculum so that your students can see Catholic characters dealing with life's problems in a way that reflects the Catholic values your school hopes to instill? Search it out! Visit websites like www.catholicteenbooks. com. Join the Facebook group Books for Catholic Teens and (shameless plug here) follow the Instagram account of the same name, which I run in order to help spread the news that there really are exciting novels with Catholic characters written by Catholic authors.

Finding new novels to read with your students, whether you teach reading or are incorporating historical fiction into your social studies lessons, will reenergize your teaching. While working on this book, I was introduced to the middle-grade novel *Ghost Boys*, by Jewell Parker Rhodes. It's a great story to use with middle school students to discuss racism in our country. Not only that, but there are positive references to All Saints' Day and the Day of the Dead in this secular book. Whenever

I find a valuable new book like this, it fuels my fire to get back into the classroom. Don't be afraid to try new things.

Have Your Sickle Handy

As I was reading through Jesus's parables, I came across the parable of the growing seed. It can be helpful to remember that sometimes our teaching is like that growing seed:

> He also said, "The kingdom of God is as if someone would scatter seed on the ground, and would sleep and rise night and day, and the seed would sprout and grow, he does not know how. The earth produces of itself, first the stalk, then the head, then the full grain in the head. But when the grain is ripe, at once he goes in with his sickle, because the harvest has come." (Mk 4:26–29)

This parable sheds light on two aspects of teaching. First, teachers are not the only ones responsible for the education of the children in their care. When a seed is planted, it needs other things to grow. It needs the earth, sunlight, and water. When we teach, we plant seeds in the minds and hearts of our students, but someone had to come before us to prepare the soil. Others will come after us to provide the sunshine and the water. And sometimes, we'll be the one providing the sunshine or watering the seed that a previous teacher or a child's parents planted. Either way, we must not get discouraged because we don't see the end product. Our contribution might seem small, but we have to trust that it will grow to fruition in time. Sometimes how this happens is just as mysterious as my cherry tomato plant suddenly sprouting twenty new tomatoes overnight!

Second, we need to remember that sometimes we *will* be there when the harvest is ready—and that's when we need to grab our sickles and reap the harvest! Don't let my imagery alarm you. I'm talking about making use of those teachable moments, those moments when a student's mind is ripe for learning. All the preparatory work has been done, and a situation presents itself that can be turned into a lesson that is ready to be learned. Sometimes these moments come in expected ways. For example, a student may keep making the same mistake in their work, and after a brief discussion, you root out the cause of the error in their thinking. Then comes the moment when the student is ready to unravel the knot and absorb the information in a way that makes sense.

Other times, these moments come unexpectedly. At one of the Catholic schools where I taught, we had special lunch outings once a month for kids who did not receive any disciplinary referrals during the previous month. It was a small school, and several fast-food places lay within walking distance, so this was a feasible adventure that the students looked forward to.

One year, I had an exceptionally small homeroom with just a few girls and a group of boys who were notorious for getting disciplinary referrals during recess for their rough play or disrespect of the rules. So one day, I found myself taking just the group of girls to lunch. I let them discuss whatever they wanted as we feasted on our special lunches. Eventually, the talk fell to how some girls in school treated other girls. Sort of your typical "mean girl" stories that come out whenever a middle school girl gets jealous of another girl. They were concerned and saddened by some of the hurt feelings between other girls at school.

Wanting to comfort them, I told them about how I had often felt "less than" as a girl at school. I wasn't popular or cool by any means, but I had a small group of friends that I could rely on. Years passed, and I had the opportunity to see and visit with some of my old classmates. To my surprise, a girl I thought had always looked down on me was actually very nice! We had more in common than I realized. While we never became close friends, I did grow to see her in a completely different way, and she is someone I would truly wish the best for. The stuff I had thought was important and that had driven a wedge between us when we were younger really wasn't important at all. Those cliques you experience in school aren't going to matter when you're older. Not if you mature.

As we got up to leave at the end of the meal, a businessman seated at the next table over stopped me. "I'm sorry for eavesdropping," he said, "but I couldn't help but overhear what you said to those girls. It was really great, that lesson you taught them. I think that's really important for young girls to hear."

I was a bit embarrassed to discover someone had overheard our conversation, but then I felt glad. That man helped me realize I had transformed a fun lunch into a teachable moment, one with an important message I hope those girls took with them into high school and beyond.

Be ready for those teachable moments. Have your sickles handy! You never know when God is going to use you to work the truly important lessons into your students' school days.

Yesterday Is Not Today

To me, one of the most frustrating things about teaching occurs when you think you've finally got it figured out. You've taught the same lesson for a few years, and you've worked out all the kinks. It's a no-fail lesson now—until the moment when it suddenly fails, and you're standing there stumped. Why didn't it work with *this* group of kids? Did I do something differently?

There could be many reasons why a lesson that has worked in the past suddenly bombs. Perhaps you did do something another way this time, and that made all the difference. Or maybe this year's group of students don't have the background knowledge that your previous classes had, and so they can't quite grasp the new ideas. Whatever the reason, there is no point in beating yourself up. Remember these wise words from Jesus: "And no one puts new wine into old wineskins; otherwise, the wine will burst the skins, and the wine is lost, and so are the skins; but one puts new wine into fresh wineskins" (Mk 2:22).

Sometimes your old lessons simply won't work. If that happens, find some new wineskins! In other words, find a new approach. It's okay to try something new when your old method is worn out.

REFLECTION QUESTIONS

1. How have you used storytelling in your teaching?
2. Take some time to examine the stories (both fiction and nonfiction) that are part of your curriculum. Do they meet the educational needs of your students? How might you reignite your teaching by adding in a new story?
3. When has an always-reliable lesson failed you? What did you learn from that experience?

EIGHT

Jesus Took Challenges in Stride

I don't need to tell you how challenging a job teaching is. I didn't write this book to discuss whether or not teaching is challenging, or even whether it will ever cease to be challenging for you. (Spoiler alert: I still find it formidable after more than twenty years in the classroom.) Even when you've taught for many years and certain aspects of teaching become less daunting, new challenges continually arise. Therefore, the focus must be on how you will respond to those challenges. Your ability to cope with challenges will impact whether you burn out or persevere.

Getting Rejected

Sometimes your students will flat out reject what you have to say. I don't know if this happens much at the elementary level, but you can be sure that some of the older students will question what they are being taught. In a way, that can be good. We want our students to be critical thinkers. On the other hand, it can be frustrating. Multiple degrees in your content area, years of experience, and the awards you may have for the work you've done won't give you immunity. You may still find a student arguing with you over whether *feel* is a linking verb as well as an action verb.

I've known a number of teachers who take this sort of confrontation personally, but I think one of the keys to surviving as a teacher is not seeing a student's rejection of something you've said as a reflection on who you are as a person or as an educator. It could be that student is belligerent with everyone. Maybe she argues just to be heard because no one listens to her at home. Maybe she argues because she struggles with self-esteem and wants to sound smart so she'll feel good about herself. Maybe she argues because someone else taught her something different and she's clinging to that misinformation she received earlier. That someone else might even be her own parent!

No matter what may cause a student to reject your teaching, remember that Jesus was rejected and questioned, too. Even his hometown provoked controversy for some people. Remember what happened when Philip went to tell his friend Nathanael about Jesus?

> The next day Jesus decided to go to Galilee. He found Philip and said to him, "Follow me." Now Philip was from Bethsaida, the city of Andrew and Peter. Philip found Nathanael and said to him, "We have found him about whom Moses in the law and also the prophets wrote, Jesus son of Joseph from Nazareth." Nathanael said to him, "Can anything good come out of Nazareth?" (Jn 1:43–46)

Nathanael did not trust that the one the prophets had written about could possibly come from a small, worthless town such as Nazareth. Did he think Philip was trying to deceive him?
Unclean spirits questioned Jesus, too.

> Just then there was in their synagogue a man with an unclean spirit, and he cried out, "What have you to do with us, Jesus of Nazareth? Have you come to destroy us? I know who you are, the Holy One of God." But Jesus rebuked him, saying, "Be silent, and come out of him!" And the unclean spirit, convulsing him and crying with a loud voice, came out of him. (Mk 1:23–26)

Even though the unclean spirit recognizes Jesus as the Holy One of God, it still challenges what Jesus is about to do. I've heard teachers complain, "Why don't my students trust me?" or "Don't they know I'm the teacher and they should listen to me?" I get the frustration. Still, it's important to remember that not everything is about us. Our students are simply trying to make sense out of the world, and let's face it, our world can be scary and confusing. Sometimes what we are teaching disrupts the little bit of order our students thought they had in their lives. That's confusing and frightening to them.

During my first year of teaching, I taught high school juniors. One day we were discussing the media and the different kinds of biases that exist in the field of journalism. When I mentioned that it was good to check for biases and prejudices in news reporting (this was well before "fake news" became a popular phrase), a girl responded with a huff, "Well, I was raised to *trust* everything I see on TV." I almost fell over. This girl was actually offended at the idea of questioning what she heard on television. To make matters worse, she had been *taught* to trust all news reports without questioning. It was hard to contradict what her parents had told her without making her parents look naive. Of course children want to believe that their parents are correct and know all the answers. (Well, at least until they are old enough to start thinking their parents don't know anything at all!)

A similar situation happened years later when I was teaching sixth grade. We were reading about mesas, the land formations that look like tables, and the students were baffled by my pronunciation. I said the word with a long *a* sound in the first syllable. They insisted that the first syllable was pronounced like the word *mess*. Finally, I asked them why they thought that, and they explained that a previous teacher had pronounced it that way. Well, of course that would make them question my pronunciation. They had learned to say the word a different way from another teacher whom they had completely trusted and respected. Could it possibly be that their beloved fourth-grade teacher had made a mistake? We looked up the word together in a dictionary and had a little discussion about using the pronunciation guide in the dictionary (see the previous chapter about taking advantage of teachable moments). Of course, nowadays a quick Google search lets us listen to the pronunciation of words.

My point is that you are going to get questions that might feel like rejections or dismissals of your intelligence and your training. Do like Jesus did. He didn't stop preaching because people questioned his hometown or spirits rebelled against his authority. He did what he was sent to do anyway. Do the same. Take those questioning moments and turn them into teachable moments. Ask students *why* they believe they are right and you are wrong. Search together for evidence for both sides of the argument and let the students come to a conclusion based on what they find.

When Your Students Drive You Crazy

Have you ever felt like your students might push you over the edge? I think Jesus used to get frustrated at times, too. In fact, there's a great line in episode 8 of the first season of the TV show *The Chosen* that reflects this idea. (If you don't know about *The Chosen* yet, I highly recommend it, and you can watch it for free online!)

As the disciples are traveling from Capernaum through Samaria, they question Jesus about why they are walking through a land they are convinced is very dangerous. They beg Jesus to take the safer route around Samaria even if it doubles their travel time. They hurl so many objections at Jesus that finally he says, "If we are going to have a question-and-answer session every time we do something you're not used to, it's going to be a very annoying time together for all of us."[7] This line makes me laugh every time I watch that episode because I want to say the same thing to *my* students sometimes. "If you are going to question me every time I ask you to use Times New Roman size 12 when you type an essay, this is going to be a very annoying year for all of us!"

While *The Chosen* may be biblical fiction, and the line above was completely made up by the show's writers, there is plenty of biblical evidence that Jesus became annoyed with his disciples from time to time. Take, for example, the healing of a boy with a spirit in chapter 9 of Mark's gospel.

> When they came to the disciples, they saw a great crowd around them, and some scribes arguing with them. When the whole crowd saw him, they were immediately overcome with awe, and they ran

> forward to greet him. He asked them, "What are you
> arguing about with them?" Someone from the crowd
> answered him, "Teacher, I brought you my son; he
> has a spirit that makes him unable to speak; and
> whenever it seizes him, it dashes him down; and he
> foams and grinds his teeth and becomes rigid; and I
> asked your disciples to cast it out, but they could not
> do so." He answered them, "You faithless generation,
> how much longer must I be among you? How much
> longer must I put up with you? Bring him to me."
> (Mk 9:14–19)

Notice that the person from the crowd first asked the disciples
to heal the boy, but they had failed. In response, Jesus calls his
disciples a "faithless generation." As we see time and time again
in the gospels, people are healed by their faith. If the disciples
had believed, perhaps they could have healed the boy. Their lack
of faith exasperates Jesus so much that he asks how much longer
he must be stuck hanging around with them before they get it.
Yikes! And he doesn't just say it once; he repeats it.

What does Jesus do then? Does he throw in the towel, or
walk away in a huff, saying, "Figure it out yourselves"? No. He
simply says, "Bring him to me." He decides to heal the boy and
model for them—once again!—how it's done. We must do likewise. Even when we're wondering how much longer we need to
work with our students before they get it and we're muttering,
"Sweet Jesus, is it June yet?" under our breath.

Sometimes, even our constant rephrasing, reteaching, and
reimagining of our lessons won't be enough. That's when I like
to remember the end of this story: "When he had entered the
house, his disciples asked him privately, 'Why could we not cast
it out?' He said to them, 'This kind can come out only through
prayer'" (Mk 9:28–29). When you've reached the end of your
rope (or run out of ideas on how to reach your students), it's a

good time to pause and pray. Ask the Lord to show you the next step to take. Ask him for patience to keep trying. Ask the Holy Spirit to fill you with wisdom, and then follow his lead.

You're Going to Fail and That's Okay

Raise your hand if you suffer from perfectionism. I know I do. It's so hard when you want to get it all right (and by "all right," I don't mean "okay"; I mean, 100 percent correct), yet your best efforts fail. St. Peter can be a comforting companion when that happens. He definitely did not get things correct 100 percent of the time. He often messed up, and not just with little mistakes. Huge mistakes!

> While Peter was below in the courtyard, one of the servant-girls of the high priest came by. When she saw Peter warming himself, she stared at him and said, "You also were with Jesus, the man from Nazareth." But he denied it, saying, "I do not know or understand what you are talking about." And he went out into the forecourt. Then the cock crowed. And the servant-girl, on seeing him, began again to say to the bystanders, "This man is one of them." But again he denied it. Then after a little while the bystanders again said to Peter, "Certainly you are one of them; for you are a Galilean." But he began to curse, and he swore an oath, "I do not know this man you are talking about." At that moment the cock crowed for the second time. Then Peter remembered that Jesus had said to him, "Before the cock crows

twice, you will deny me three times." And he broke
down and wept. (Mk 14:66–72)

Ouch! I cringe every time I read this passage. Peter didn't mess
up just once or twice. At *the* most critical moment, he denied
knowing Jesus three times! To make matters worse, Jesus had
even warned him that he was going to do it. He told Peter that it
would happen three times before the cock crowed twice. Imagine Peter's reaction when he realized what he had done. The Bible
tells us that "he went out and wept bitterly" (Lk 22:62). He must
have wanted to crawl into a hole.

When I practice imaginative prayer with this scene, I imagine Peter stumbling out of that courtyard away from the servants
and the officers. The sun is just starting to rise, and he makes his
way to a still-dark corner of the city, maybe an alleyway where
light from the rising sun hasn't crept in yet. He huddles up in
that dark space and just bawls. He had been warned! He had
sworn he wouldn't do it. But then he had! Just hours earlier, he
had cut off the ear of a soldier in the Garden of Gethsemane in
order to protect Jesus, but now he couldn't even admit that he
knew him. How quickly Peter had turned from an impulsive yet
courageous guardian to a scared follower! His heart must have
cried out in agony at how quickly he had changed under pressure
and how epically he had failed to stand up for Jesus.

Despite all this, Peter went on to lead the disciples after
Jesus's death. He became the first bishop of Rome and bravely
faced crucifixion upside down. What does this tell us? It tells us
that even when we fail as teachers, we can still find God's grace,
pick ourselves up, and try again. We can still do great things
even if we stumble sometimes. If the first pope can fail three
times in one evening and still get the job done, you can, too!

Try, Try Again

One thing I've noticed in my study of the gospels is that Jesus performs the same miracles more than once. He doesn't heal only one person; he heals many, many people. He doesn't drive demons out of Mary Magdalene alone; he drives demons out of multiple other people as well.

I don't remember what age I was, but I was well into my teaching career when I finally figured out that there were *two* gospel stories in which Jesus multiplied loaves of bread and fish to feed a large crowd—not just the same story in the different gospels. Both Matthew and Mark share two different times during which Jesus worked a miracle in order to feed thousands of people.

In Matthew's gospel, the first account appears in the middle of chapter 14 and is called "Feeding the Five Thousand." This event occurs right after John the Baptist has been beheaded. Such a violent end to his cousin's ministry could have easily scared a normal human into abandoning his own ministry, and to be fair, Jesus does try to sneak away by himself, but the crowds follow him.

> Now when Jesus heard this, he withdrew from there in a boat to a deserted place by himself. But when the crowds heard it, they followed him on foot from the towns. When he went ashore, he saw a great crowd; and he had compassion for them and cured their sick. When it was evening, the disciples came to him and said, "This is a deserted place, and the hour is now late; send the crowds away so that they may go into the villages and buy food for themselves." Jesus said to them, "They need not go away; you give them something to eat." They replied, "We have nothing here but five loaves and two fish." And he said, "Bring

them here to me." Then he ordered the crowds to sit
down on the grass. Taking the five loaves and the two
fish, he looked up to heaven, and blessed and broke
the loaves, and gave them to the disciples, and the
disciples gave them to the crowds. And all ate and
were filled; and they took up what was left over of the
broken pieces, twelve baskets full. And those who ate
were about five thousand men, besides women and
children. (Mt 14:13–21)

Note that Jesus did not turn away the sick people who followed
him hoping for a cure to their illness, even though he had wanted to go off on his own for a while. I try to remember this passage whenever a student wants to see me for extra help during
lunch or before school or after school. Sometimes, we crave a bit
of downtime. There's nothing wrong with that. Teaching has us
"on stage" so much, and if you're an introvert like me, you can
only recharge when you're alone. However, sometimes students
really need a little extra help. When you're weary but a student
needs you, ask Jesus to send you strength. He knows what it's
like to be tired, to want to be alone for a bit, yet still be moved
with compassion to help those who need it.

The second story of multiplying loaves of bread and fish
falls at the end of the next chapter and is called "Feeding the
Four Thousand." What happens in between is a series of other
miracles. Jesus walked on water, he healed many people at
Gennesaret, he drove a demon out of a Canaanite woman's
daughter, and then he cured even more people on a mountain
near the Sea of Galilee. I'm exhausted just reading that list!

The people who followed him up on the mountain stayed
with him for days. They didn't want to leave, and Jesus didn't
make them. Instead, he performed a reprise of his previous
miracle.

> Then Jesus called his disciples to him and said, "I
> have compassion for the crowd, because they have
> been with me now for three days and have nothing
> to eat; and I do not want to send them away hungry,
> for they might faint on the way." The disciples said to
> him, "Where are we to get enough bread in the desert
> to feed so great a crowd?" Jesus asked them, "How
> many loaves have you?" They said, "Seven, and a few
> small fish." Then ordering the crowd to sit down on
> the ground, he took the seven loaves and the fish; and
> after giving thanks he broke them and gave them
> to the disciples, and the disciples gave them to the
> crowds. And all of them ate and were filled; and they
> took up the broken pieces left over, seven baskets
> full. Those who had eaten were four thousand men,
> besides women and children. After sending away the
> crowds, he got into the boat and went to the region
> of Magadan. (Mt 15:32–39)

Why repeat the same miracle? Because the people needed it,
of course! And that's what we have to remember when we are
asked to repeat the same lesson or the same instructions over
and over again. Our students need it, in the same way that the
group of four thousand needed food even though the group of
five thousand (some of whom might have been the same people)
had been fed previously.

Jesus didn't stop and ask, "How many miracles do you people need?!" He just kept working miracles. How many lesson
plans bordering on the miraculous do our students need? As
many as it takes! I'm reminded of one of my Catholic schools
where I taught the same students three years in a row. The first
year I tried to explain all the grammar lessons the best I could.
I thought I had been really thorough, so the next year when I
taught them again, I thought I wouldn't have to repeat much.
Instead, I grew discouraged when lessons intended to just be

refreshers came across like new material to the students. I'm sure we've all been there. You *know* that the previous teacher taught them a certain concept, but now they act like they've never heard of it.

Finally, this group of students and I got to our third year in a row of being together. I braced myself to go into a full description of direct objects and indirect objects once again. Just to humor myself, I asked the class, "Anybody remember anything about direct objects?"

A girl rattled off a perfect explanation.

Oh good, I thought, *at least one person was listening.* "Okay, well, how about an indirect object?"

A different student rattled off another perfect explanation. I asked a few more probing questions and discovered that lo and behold, they remembered it! It might have taken until the third year, but they really got it! No questions, no guessing games about which words were direct objects and which were indirect objects. My point? Don't be afraid to try again and again, and don't be discouraged. It will sink in eventually.

The Agony in the Classroom

You don't have to teach for very long before something happens in your classroom that brings you to your knees crying. For me, the first time was during my student teaching. Thankfully, I didn't cry in front of the class, but I cried in the car on the drive back to my college apartment.

My first year of teaching brought more tears. You might recall from chapter 2 that this was the year I had a student arrested for gang activity and another student who had watched her friend die in her arms. In addition to that, a few of the other students that year seemed to downright hate me. I had had students during my student teaching who gave me some disciplinary issues, but those kids just seemed mischievous. I didn't take their misbehavior personally. These kids, on the other hand, seemed to loathe me. There have been numerous agonizing moments over the years, times when I felt abandoned by God and wondered if I'd made a mistake in choosing a teaching career.

When we feel like God has abandoned us, it's good to remember that Jesus felt abandoned, too. Take, for instance, the Agony in the Garden:

> They went to a place called Gethsemane; and he said to his disciples, "Sit here while I pray." He took with him Peter and James and John, and began to be distressed and agitated. And he said to them, "I am deeply grieved, even to death; remain here, and keep awake." And going a little farther, he threw himself on the ground and prayed that, if it were possible, the hour might pass from him. He said, "Abba, Father, for you all things are possible; remove this cup from me; yet, not what I want, but what you want." He came and found them sleeping; and he said to Peter, "Simon, are you asleep? Could you not keep awake one hour? Keep awake and pray that you may not come into the time of trial; the spirit indeed is willing, but the flesh is weak." And again he went away and prayed, saying the same words. And once more he came and found them sleeping, for their eyes were very heavy; and they did not know what to say to him. He came a third time and said to them, "Are you still sleeping and taking your rest? Enough! The hour has come; the Son of Man is betrayed into the hands of sinners. Get up, let us be going. See, my betrayer is at hand." (Mk 14:32–42)

Jesus knows what it's like to be greatly troubled and distressed. Notice what he does during this time. He goes off and prays. He brings some of his friends so that they might pray with him, which is a good reminder for us as well. When we struggle in our day-to-day teaching, it's good to ask others to pray with and for us.

I think that this is probably one of the most beautiful things about teaching at a Catholic school. Prayer is built right into your day. You pray with the students in the morning, usually before or after you recite the Pledge of Allegiance. You pray with the entire student body and staff during school Masses. Your principal probably starts your faculty and team meetings with prayer. What a beautiful thing! Don't take it for granted. And don't forget to bring the challenges you are facing into those prayer opportunities. If it's appropriate, name your intention when there is a chance to do so. But also don't underestimate the whispered prayers in our hearts. Prayer doesn't have to be formal, and it doesn't have to be said aloud. It can be that longing in your heart when you ask for the Lord's help wordlessly as you face a student who is being belligerent toward you or hurtful to a classmate. When you're ready to lose your temper, try repeating the Jesus prayer in your head ("Lord Jesus Christ, Son of God, have mercy on me, a sinner") as you take a deep breath. Or make a quick call for the Holy Spirit to come into the situation: "*Veni, Sancte Spiritus!*" ("Come, Holy Spirit!")

Listen, I'm not going to lie to you. It has taken me years to get used to the idea of offering up silent prayers while teaching. When we are in the thick of things in the classroom, prayer might be the furthest thing from our minds. However, I have found that when I do remember to take a breath and offer up a quick plea for help from God, I am always heard. He has never failed me. When I ask for help in deciding what to say to a child I need to discipline or an angry parent whose call I am about to return, I immediately think of a better explanation or phrasing than I would've come up with on my own. And even though I am getting better at asking for God's help in the classroom, it's still a practice I'm working on.

And when I say I'm working on it, I mean it's really hard work. At one point in my teaching career, I fell into a "Garden of Gethsemane" period. I was coming home and crying almost every night. I had been asked to teach six different lessons every day and was overworked and exhausted. The materials were all new for both the reading and the language arts classes I was teaching, which meant that I couldn't fall back on any old lesson plans or even use the lesson plans of the teacher from the previous year. Furthermore, in addition to all of the new lesson planning that was required, I was also being asked to take some graduate-level courses because of the new position I had been moved into. Every day I walked into school ready to quit my job. I got through the day by telling myself, *I only have to teach today. I can quit tomorrow.*

Yep, it was *that* bad.

To give myself a little hope, I decided that when I did quit teaching (which I was becoming more convinced was the thing to do with each passing day), I would start a new career doing something that made me happy: baking. I started looking for schools that offered a degree or certification for being a pastry chef. My online search led me to Kendall College, one of the top culinary schools in Chicago. When I noticed they had an upcoming open house, I registered and attended. That evening, I sat in an educational space with people much, much younger than I and listened to talks about financial assistance and admissions. Mind you, I had finished my master's degree in language arts instruction at this time and had paid off all my student loans while teaching. Then I walked through the instructional rooms as the teachers talked about how classes would run from 5:00

p.m. until about 11:00 p.m. two nights a week, but we should be prepared to stay later than 11:00 p.m. because sometimes cakes take longer to bake and decorate than you expect, and then there's the cleanup.

My mind whirled. How was I going to teach the next day if I was in class until nearly midnight and then had to drive forty-five minutes home?

So I sat with the idea for a while, and I listened to friends who told me of others they knew who had gone to pastry-chef school. Did I really want to wake up well before dawn each morning? Most bakeries are open early, and the bakers have to get things going even earlier. How did I feel about lugging around fifty-pound bags of flour? Baking cute little cupcakes in your kitchen is one thing. Using industrial-size mixers is another.

Obviously, I never became a pastry chef, and baking went back to being a hobby for me. However, I tell you this story because I want to be honest about just how dark my "Garden of Gethsemane" time became. I nearly walked away from education—and at a point when most people who are going to leave teaching have already done so. Those who decide teaching is not for them usually exit within the first five years. I nearly quit after more than a decade in the profession.

How have I persevered? Through prayer and by the grace of God. Teacher burnout is real, and it can strike at any time. Build up your prayer fortress, my friends. And when you find yourself in your own Garden of Gethsemane, remember that you are not alone. Jesus may have been abandoned by his friends, but he will not abandon you.

REFLECTION QUESTIONS

1. How have you been humbled in your work as a teacher, and how has that humbling caused you to grow as an educator?
2. In what ways do you relate to St. Peter?
3. How do you deal with the frustration of students forgetting something you know they have been taught?
4. Recall the darkest period in your teaching career. What kept you going?

NINE

Jesus Trusted God's Grace to Do Divine Arithmetic

I'm a big fan of Catholic musician Matt Maher. In 2003, feeling burned out from his work in parish ministry, Matt penned the song "Your Grace Is Enough," which is inspired by 2 Corinthians 12:9 ("My grace is sufficient for you").[8] Let's look at this line in the context of St. Paul's second letter to the Corinthians.

> Therefore, to keep me from being too elated, a thorn was given me in the flesh, a messenger of Satan to torment me, to keep me from being too elated. Three times I appealed to the Lord about this, that it would

leave me, but he said to me, "My grace is sufficient
for you, for power is made perfect in weakness." So,
I will boast all the more gladly of my weaknesses,
so that the power of Christ may dwell in me. (2 Cor
12:7–9)

Although we don't know the exact nature of his "thorn in the
flesh," St. Paul says that it kept him from becoming too excited
or boastful over the work he was doing for the Lord. He asked
God several times to remove the thorn, but God answered that
his grace was enough to sustain Paul.

Sometimes I think that I can only be successful if there are
no thorns in my side. If the path is totally clear and I have no
cause to stumble, then all will be well. However, that's not true.
Thorns grow. Stumbling blocks appear. Doors are slammed in
my face. The good news is that we need not worry. God's grace
is enough to get us through it. In fact, the Lord told St. Paul
that "power is made perfect in weakness." So the next time you
feel discouraged because your teaching isn't going as smoothly
as you'd like, remember that God's grace will be enough to get
you through it. And if that doesn't work, then crank up Matt
Maher's song. It always makes me feel better!

Sow the Seeds and Then Trust in God

In chapter 7, we reflected on the parable of the sower. Let's consider that parable again, but add to it some of the lessons from
the Sermon on the Mount, particularly the part where Jesus tells
his followers not to worry about the future.

> Therefore I tell you, do not worry about your life,
> what you will eat or what you will drink, or about
> your body, what you will wear. Is not life more than
> food, and the body more than clothing? Look at the
> birds of the air; they neither sow nor reap nor gather
> into barns, and yet your heavenly Father feeds them.
> Are you not of more value than they? And can any
> of you by worrying add a single hour to your span of
> life? And why do you worry about clothing? Consider
> the lilies of the field, how they grow; they neither
> toil nor spin, yet I tell you, even Solomon in all his
> glory was not clothed like one of these. But if God
> so clothes the grass of the field, which is alive today
> and tomorrow is thrown into the oven, will he not
> much more clothe you—you of little faith? Therefore
> do not worry, saying, "What will we eat?" or "What
> will we drink?" or "What will we wear?" For it is the
> Gentiles who strive for all these things; and indeed
> your heavenly Father knows that you need all these
> things. But strive first for the kingdom of God and
> his righteousness, and all these things will be given
> to you as well. (Mt 6:25–33)

I can be a worrier, especially when that Cattapanalysis Paralysis
sets in. What if I make the wrong decision about what book to
read with my students or how to respond to that contentious
email?

To put it in terms of the parable of the sower, I worry that
I'll sow a bunch of "seeds" in my students, and none of them
will grow at all! In fact, sometimes I think it's a miracle that
any seeds grow. There are so many things that can go wrong
after you plant a seed. So it is with our teaching as well. Many
things can inhibit our lessons from taking root in our students.
Sometimes they are like the seeds sown on the path. Something
prevents our students from understanding right from the start,

and we "lose" them immediately. Sometimes our lessons are like the seeds among the rocks. Our students seem to understand the lesson at first but can't make the connections necessary for deep understanding; the lesson doesn't take root in them. Some of our lessons are like the seeds sown among thorns. The students hear what we are trying to impart, but other things pull them away. They focus on issues that are more pressing to them at the moment. As a middle school teacher, I've lost the attention of students for various reasons—some may be temporarily distracted by a friend who has hurt them, while others have serious concerns such as worrying about a parent who is terminally ill.

At the same time that we admit that we can't control many aspects of our students' lives, we should remember that God's grace is still enough. He cares for us and for our students even more than he cares for the birds of the air and the lilies of the field. After all, some of the seeds do fall on good soil. They not only take root and grow, but even bear fruit one hundredfold! God can take the seeds we plant and make them grow into something way beyond our expectations. We need to trust that he will make good with those seeds in his own time.

God's time may be much later than we expect. One day, after a particularly frustrating day of teaching, I headed out of the school building about an hour after the students had left. It had taken me that long to get at least the basics ready for the next day's lessons, and I carried home a tote bag filled with papers to grade. When I stepped outside, I saw some older students hanging around the bus lane. A few were on bikes; some were just standing there. They weren't our eighth graders. They looked to be high school students. Sure enough, one of the girls moved away from the others and called out my name. As she ran toward me, I recognized her as a girl I had taught in eighth grade two years earlier. My heart rate sped up a bit. She had been the kind of girl to roll her eyes every now and then in class. I was pretty sure I hadn't been her favorite teacher.

"Ms. Cattapan," she called, as I made an effort to avoid eye contact and make my way to the parking lot without being noticed. "Ms. Cattapan, wait up!"

I stopped and braced myself. Everything in my gut told me this was going to be an awkward conversation at best. No teacher minds seeing past students they *know* liked them, but when it's a former student who disliked you, that's another story.

"Hi, how are you? How's high school?" I asked, trying not to betray my worry about where this conversation would go.

"Oh good. Well, okay, I guess. I mean, I just wanted to thank you."

"Thank me?"

"Yeah, I mean, the two English teachers I've had in high school, well, they're just not very good, and I keep thinking about how good you were. I think you were, like, one of the best English teachers I've ever had. I learned so much from you. I didn't realize it then, but I get it now."

You could have knocked me over with a feather. Here I was thinking that nothing I had taught this girl had made a difference. I was certain she hadn't even liked me, much less learned anything from me, and now she was thanking me for how much I had taught her. I had planted seeds and God had taken care of the rest. His grace was sufficient to finish the job.

We plant seeds, and often we think we've failed. However, that might only be because we aren't around when those seeds finally bear fruit. If you're lucky, maybe a few times in your career a student from the past will come back and thank you for what you did. It may even be a student you were convinced had not learned a single thing in your classroom. They might not even have realized how much you taught them at first. Think about the teachers you had as a student. Did you always appreciate them in the moment? Were there some teachers whose wisdom you didn't truly come to understand until you'd had a few more years to grow into your own wisdom?

During my doctoral studies, I came across the following quote that helps explain why it can be so hard to stay in the teaching game: "The opportunity to be effective is the single most powerful motivator for entering and staying in teaching and for triggering commitment and effort."[9] If we want to teach because we believe we can be effective, then not getting to see how effective we are makes it more challenging to remain motivated. Our brains keep track of effort versus effect. Putting in a lot of effort and seeing little effect zaps our motivation. We don't feel like what we're doing is worth it anymore. That's when we burn out. So what can we do to combat that?

One thing I've tried is looking at *how* I am working as a teacher. Are there things I am putting lots of effort into that could be done more efficiently? For example, let's say I'm reading a student's essay and that student keeps forgetting to capitalize the pronoun "I." Maybe I can stop marking every single instance of it on the page. Instead, I can add a comment about it once and tell the student to look through the essay and correct the rest on their own.

If I have a ton of things to grade and I'm feeling overwhelmed, I can look critically at the different types of assignments. Can any of them be graded quickly without a taxing amount of thought, like a spelling test? I might choose to do those first. I'll feel like I've accomplished something quickly and my effort has been worth it. More challenging assignments, like essay grading, need to be broken into chunks. I set myself a goal, perhaps ten essays a day, and then find a time and place where I can truly focus on them and not get distracted. The more distracted I am, the longer it will take, and the less I'll feel like my effort is getting the results I want.

Another trick I've used is to reassess my goal. Do I expect all my students to turn into award-winning novelists? No. Maybe my original goal was to get them all to write perfect persuasive essays, but then I realize that my goal needs to be adjusted to understanding basic paragraphing structure. We can focus on being persuasive after we've mastered what makes a group of sentences into a paragraph.

I think one of the hardest things we as teachers face is the fact that we are like farmers who plant seeds but rarely get to reap the harvest. If you are fortunate to teach in a small school (which most Catholic schools are), think about ways you as a faculty member can share success stories of kids who have moved on to the upper grades. This can be one of the unexpected bonuses of assigning older students to younger students as buddies. The primary-grade teachers can see firsthand what the older students are like now as they work with their younger buddies, and the middle school and upper-elementary teachers can see their future students while they are still young.

Never Underestimate Your Mustard Seed

Mustard seeds are only one or two millimeters in diameter, yet the trees they produce grow from six to twenty feet high, and their width can stretch to twenty feet as well. Some mustard trees have even grown to thirty feet high. The kind of mustard tree Jesus would have known in the Middle East had adapted to its arid climate. It grew despite bad soil, little rainfall, and extreme heat. Imagine such a large and hardy plant starting from such a small beginning.

> He put before them another parable: "The kingdom
> of heaven is like a mustard seed that someone took
> and sowed in his field; it is the smallest of all the
> seeds, but when it has grown it is the greatest of
> shrubs and becomes a tree, so that the birds of the air
> come and make nests in its branches." (Mt 13:31–32)

The people of Jesus's time would have been very familiar with a mustard seed and its plant, so they didn't require an explanation of this parable. For us as teachers, it can serve as a reminder that the tiny seeds we plant in our students can take hold and grow into something sturdy despite the harsh conditions our students might face. Not only can such seeds grow into something magnificent for that student, but they might also have a lasting impact on others. Note that at the end of this brief parable, Jesus points out that the birds make their nests in the tree. That tiny seed didn't just grow for its own benefit. It grew for the benefit of the birds as well.

Two parallel examples from the world of education come to mind. As I mentioned earlier, as a teen I taught Sunday school to four-year-olds at my parish, where my mom ran the pre-school Sunday school program. The teachers were often high school students, and the helpers were middle school students or young high school students who hadn't taken over their own classrooms yet. When I look back on my fellow Sunday school teachers, I know that many of them decided to study education in college and went on to become classroom teachers. Think of what my mother did by running this program. Obviously, she helped bring the faith to some of the youngest members of our parish (and gave their parents a chance to attend Mass in peace while their child received an age-appropriate religion lesson). However, my mom's impact reached much further than that. She raised up a generation of teachers who then went on to support far more students in their own classrooms.

What about my own reach as a teacher? How many of my former students have gone on to become teachers because of me? To be honest, I have no idea. I remember one former student at St. Philip the Apostle School who looked around in wonder at my room and said, "Ms. Cattapan, when I become a teacher, I want to organize my room like yours. Everything is so organized!" I laugh now when I think of it because my room seems to become less organized the longer I teach, and I note that some of my younger colleagues are much more organized than I am!

I don't know if that girl grew up to be a teacher, but I did hear from another former student who did. And that was another definite surprise. He found my author page on Facebook and messaged me. First, he wanted to confirm that I was the same Ms. Cattapan who had taught at St. Anastasia School. When I recognized his name and confirmed that I was, he informed me that he was a middle school English teacher now, too. The shocking part was that he had nearly failed my class the first quarter of eighth grade. He was a very bright boy with a sharp wit and great writing skills; he just didn't see the point in doing his work. I remember how upset his dad was during parent-teacher fall conferences. I said something about being able to tell he was bright from the little bit of work I saw, but I couldn't be sure *just how bright* he was unless I saw more work from him! The father began weekly check-ins with the teachers, and the boy started turning in his work. Not surprisingly, his grades shot up.

Years later, when he contacted me on Facebook, he made a crack about how he was now teaching middle school and karma was getting him back for the way he had behaved when he was that age! I laughed, but I often think that he's probably doing a fabulous job. He knows from firsthand experience why some kids don't turn in their work, and I'm betting he's using that knowledge to plant his own mustard seeds.

Not too many years ago, I was serving dinner at a local soup kitchen when a young man walked up to me and introduced himself. I smiled and shook his hand. Then he went on to explain, "I think you were my eighth-grade English teacher." Suddenly, the name and the face clicked. I had indeed been his eighth-grade teacher, and now here he was—nearly ten years later—all grown up and highly involved in the running of this soup kitchen. I had taught him at a public school, and this was a soup kitchen run through a Catholic organization, so I couldn't take any credit in encouraging him to do work like this, but clearly someone had. Whether this young man had been volunteering at the soup kitchen for a long time or a short time, someone planted the seed of that idea in his head. The seed took hold and grew. I began to see him every time I came in for my monthly volunteer slot. Whoever had originally given him the idea to volunteer there hadn't just impacted his life; they had impacted the lives of everyone who came through that soup kitchen.

Don't underestimate the mustard seeds you plant. They will grow and turn into hardy plants that not only survive but spread out their branches to provide a resting place for others.

Your Fish Will Be Enough

Earlier I mentioned the TV show *The Chosen*. I'm going to bring it up again because the director of that show, Dallas Jenkins, often talks about bringing his "loaves and fishes," and I think it's a lesson we teachers need to learn as well. This lesson comes from the two gospel stories of the multiplication of the loaves and the fish. I shared Matthew's two accounts earlier. Let's look at Mark's account of the feeding of the five thousand now:

> As he went ashore, he saw a great crowd; and he had
> compassion for them, because they were like sheep
> without a shepherd; and he began to teach them
> many things. When it grew late, his disciples came to
> him and said, "This is a deserted place, and the hour
> is now very late; send them away so that they may go
> into the surrounding country and villages and buy
> something for themselves to eat." But he answered
> them, "You give them something to eat." They said
> to him, "Are we to go and buy two hundred denarii
> worth of bread, and give it to them to eat?" And he
> said to them, "How many loaves have you? Go and
> see." When they had found out, they said, "Five, and
> two fish." Then he ordered them to get all the people
> to sit down in groups on the green grass. So they sat
> down in groups of hundreds and of fifties. Taking the
> five loaves and the two fish, he looked up to heaven,
> and blessed and broke the loaves, and gave them to
> his disciples to set before the people; and he divided
> the two fish among them all. And all ate and were
> filled; and they took up twelve baskets full of broken
> pieces and of the fish. Those who had eaten the loaves
> numbered five thousand men. (Mk 6:34–44)

Notice that when Jesus asks his disciples to feed the people, they respond with how costly that purchase would be, as if to say, "You think we have that much money?" Clearly, the disciples do not, so Jesus asks them how many loaves they do have. The number is pitiful considering the number of people present. They have only five loaves of bread and two fish.

Sometimes in our teaching, it feels like we have very little to give our students. Maybe our resources are lacking—we're using old textbooks; we don't have the latest technology. Maybe we feel like we're not properly trained to deal with some of the educational challenges of our students, much less their mental and physical health needs. I certainly had no idea when I went into teaching that I would have to learn how to administer an EpiPen! I hadn't even heard of a peanut allergy until my second year of teaching, and I thought this parent was overreacting when she said her child could die from eating peanut butter. At the time, no one had ever heard of such a thing. Now, of course, food allergies are common, and teachers know all about EpiPens and diabetes management and how to react if a child has a seizure.

Despite all our training, it can still feel at times like we have little to offer our students or that our efforts just aren't cutting it. This is when it's good to remember what director Dallas Jenkins learned. He wanted to make a multiseason TV show about Jesus, but he didn't have (and didn't really want) the backing of a big Hollywood studio. He wanted to do this without the restrictions that Hollywood might put on him. A short film he made got him noticed by an independent studio willing to help him do the crowdfunding for his project, but he figured they would only raise about $800. He decided to show up and do his job anyway. He would offer whatever meager loaves and fish he had and leave the rest to God. Well, God multiplied the loaves and fish that Dallas and the early investors brought just as he multiplied the loaves and fish in Mark's gospel. Dallas's little TV show became the largest crowdfunded media project of all time, raising $10 million for the first season alone.

Our God is a God of miracles. Don't be afraid to show up with whatever meager supplies or ideas you have. Leave the rest to God. He can do "impossible math" as Dallas Jenkins and his wife, Amanda, put it (or "divine arithmetic," as my editor Jaymie puts it) and multiply your loaves and fish into something much larger than your imagination.

REFLECTION QUESTIONS

1. Have you ever had a moment when you were surprised by the impact you'd had on a previous student?
2. The mustard seeds you plant in your students will have far-reaching consequences. What's something you were taught by a teacher, parent, or mentor that is now having a far-reaching consequence in your life?
3. Can you think of a time when God used your meager offerings to make something much bigger than you had imagined it could be?

TEN

Jesus Knew When to Stop and Just Let It Be

Confession: I have some, but not all, of the answers when it comes to fighting teacher burnout. Many days I'm just taking it one step at a time. It's hard because I'm a control freak who would like to know exactly the next steps God wants me to take. In ways too numerous and nuanced to explain in this book (they would require a book all of their own), God has been slowly prying my fingers away from the tight grip of control I've been trying to hang onto. He keeps calling me to let go and let it be.

But what does it mean for us to just "let it be"? I think it means that we must concentrate on being what God has called us to be. And what is that? Saints, of course! The goal is eternity in heaven with God. However, the path to sainthood is different for each of us, and the best way to figure out what that means for you is to have a deep prayer life and a close relationship with Christ. It means lots of listening during prayer.

At the same time, there are certain things we can concentrate on no matter the particulars of our own circumstances. Our shared vocation as educators calls us all to certain ways of being (or becoming).

Be the Servant

During one of my doctoral classes, I was asked about my leadership style. I've always seen myself as striving to be a servant leader. We are called to be like Jesus washing the feet of his disciples. In other words, we are called to serve our students. This is summed up in Mark's gospel: "For the Son of Man came not to be served but to serve, and to give his life a ransom for many" (Mk 10:45). Thankfully, we are not required to give up our lives, but we are expected to give of ourselves for our students.

Sometimes this requires small sacrifices, like when you'd rather be watching your favorite show but you're grading those projects because you know a student is counting on that grade to remain eligible for the sport he's playing that season. Sometimes it requires bigger sacrifices, like giving up a higher-paying job opportunity outside the field of education in order to work as an educator. As I was wrapping up my student teaching, one of the other student teachers declared she wasn't even going to look for a job as a math teacher. She could get a job in an accounting office and make much more money and probably be less stressed in the process.

Sometimes teaching involves sacrificing a bit of our pride. Take, for example, the time I dressed up as a boy for a variety show. Our small Catholic school held a variety show every year with each homeroom putting on an act. This was generally a musical act that was practiced during weekly music lessons. During my first year at the school, my homeroom did a joint act with another homeroom. The other homeroom teacher was a Backstreet Boys fan and talked the music teacher into letting the students do a mash-up of a couple Backstreet Boys songs. This was a number of years ago, so the details are fading from my memory (maybe that's a grace I should be thankful for). But somehow, both the other homeroom teacher and I ended up in the act dressed as boys! She played the part of one of the Back-street Boys, along with other boys from her homeroom, and I ended up dressed like a boy when seen from the back. Halfway through the song, I turned around to reveal my true identity. I felt ridiculous, but you know what? The kids loved it! The parents got a big laugh out of it. Many thought I was one of the boys in class (it pays to be short!) until I turned around, removed the hat I was wearing, and let my long hair tumble down.

Why does any of this matter? Being in a required variety show act is not the kind of thing every middle school student is crazy about. To some, it's just boring. To others, it's embarrassing to be put on stage and forced to perform. However, with two of their teachers willing to make fools out of themselves (if memory serves me, the other teacher painted a little mustache on her face, so I got off easy!), even the reluctant kids got into the act. It turned what could have been a boring music class assignment into something they looked forward to rehearsing.

Be a Real Person

As an author who has been active on social media for years, I've seen lots of talk among other Christian authors and speakers about the importance of being authentic. I follow many of my fellow authors and speakers, and the ones that are the most fun to follow are the ones who let you see who they really are. They don't hide behind perfectly crafted photos of their books and professional shots of their speaking engagements. They show you their ups and downs. That's not to say many of us don't enjoy a good filter on Instagram to improve the lighting! But I do hope that people who follow me on social media get a sense of my real personality.

The importance of being our authentic selves when we teach came home to me when I read the gospel story of the healing of the hemorrhaging woman.

> As he went, the crowds pressed in on him. Now there was a woman who had been suffering from hemorrhages for twelve years; and though she had spent all she had on physicians, no one could cure her. She came up behind him and touched the fringe of his clothes, and immediately her hemorrhage stopped. Then Jesus asked, "Who touched me?" When all denied it, Peter said, "Master, the crowds surround you and press in on you." But Jesus said, "Someone touched me; for I noticed that power had gone out from me." When the woman saw that she could not remain hidden, she came trembling; and falling down before him, she declared in the presence of all the people why she had touched him, and how she had been immediately healed. He said to her, "Daughter, your faith has made you well; go in peace." (Lk 8:42–48)

When I read this story, I was struck that Jesus performed no physical action here as in many of his other miraculous healings. For example, in John 9:1–12, we see him spit on the ground, make mud out of his spit, and then rub it onto a man's eyes to heal his blindness. When Jesus heals the paralytic (see Luke 5:17–26), he first forgives the man's sins and then tells him to rise, pick up his mat, and walk. However, in the story of the hemorrhaging woman, Jesus doesn't do or say anything. He's just standing there. Yet the woman is healed as she touches the hem of his garment.

Jesus healed simply by being himself. Likewise, we can teach simply by being ourselves. Students can learn so much from us just by watching how we interact with others. How do we treat the new kid who transferred in the middle of the school year? Are we welcoming and friendly? How do we react when someone says something to get a rise out of us? Do we stay calm and respond in kindness? How reverent are we when we enter church? Do we participate fully in school Masses, or is it just part of the job for us?

During my early years of teaching, a more experienced coworker helped me and one of my young colleagues to appreciate the importance of simply being ourselves while teaching. My young colleague was in her early twenties, and I was probably approaching thirty at the time. The experienced coworker complimented the two of us on being role models for the middle school girls by wearing cute but modest clothes and not covering our young faces with tons of makeup. I still don't wear much makeup to school; I'm lucky if I can get on some tinted moisturizer, eyeliner, and lip balm. The thing is that it never occurred to me that my colleague and I could be teaching young girls about modesty and authentic beauty simply by being ourselves.

We tend to think our students don't pay much attention to us. To be fair, with the number of times we have to repeat instructions in class, our presumption has some grounding. However, kids do notice what we're doing—and what we're wearing! One day I had to laugh at the shocked look on the face of one of my students when I came to school in jeans for a special spirit day. She said to me, "You're wearing jeans! I can't believe it. You're always dressed in *business* pants!" Later that same year, she told me I wore too many dark colors and I needed to dress in bright colors more often.

Kids notice what we do and what we say. Wouldn't it be nice if they saw the face of Christ and heard his voice when we spoke? Those are big shoes to fill! But we are his hands and feet. If our students don't have good relationships with their parents, we might be the only adults they meet who can provide a healthy role model. The good news is that you don't really need to do anything special. Simply be the good person God is already calling you to be!

Be in the Desert (Some of the Time)

When we're feeling especially overwhelmed by our work, it is good to ask ourselves the old question "What would Jesus do?" In the gospels, the answer is simple: get away! Yes, Jesus sometimes had to withdraw from people in order to recharge. In fact, he didn't even start his mission until he had taken some time away. In Luke's gospel, this happens right after John baptizes him in the Jordan and before he begins his ministry.

> Jesus, full of the Holy Spirit, returned from the Jordan and was led by the Spirit in the wilderness, where for forty days he was tempted by the devil. He

ate nothing at all during those days, and when they were over, he was famished. The devil said to him, "If you are the Son of God, command this stone to become a loaf of bread." Jesus answered him, "It is written, 'One does not live by bread alone.'"

Then the devil led him up and showed him in an instant all the kingdoms of the world. And the devil said to him, "To you I will give their glory and all this authority; for it has been given over to me, and I give it to anyone I please. If you, then, will worship me, it will all be yours." Jesus answered him, "It is written,

> 'Worship the Lord your God,
>   and serve only him.'"

Then the devil took him to Jerusalem, and placed him on the pinnacle of the temple, saying to him, "If you are the Son of God, throw yourself down from here, for it is written,

> 'He will command his angels concerning you,
>   to protect you,'

and

> 'On their hands they will bear you up,
>   so that you will not dash your foot against
>   a stone.'"

Jesus answered him, "It is said, 'Do not put the Lord your God to the test.'" When the devil had finished every test, he departed from him until an opportune time. (Lk 4:1–13)

Note that Jesus's preparation for his teaching work isn't easy. He's tempted by the devil multiple times, but he needs to go through this time away from other people before beginning his ministry. This is good for us to remember when we need to gear up for the next semester or school year. We, too, could use some time away from others to prepare ourselves for the work we are about to do.

If you're a Catholic school principal, think about how you might add some "desert time" into your professional development days at the beginning of the school year. In other words, consider how you might build in time for the teachers to have some quiet reflection and prayer that will help them get their hearts and minds ready for the challenges ahead. This desert time, when we steal away to be with the Lord, could take the form of eucharistic adoration or time set aside for teachers to work in their classrooms on their own. Sometimes, I think administrators feel they need to schedule every moment of a professional development day so that no time is wasted. But if that time can be spent with God, then it's most definitely *not* wasted. One of my favorite professional development days ever was when the principal arranged for us to have a sort of retreat. We had some group prayer time and reflection, but we also used the rooms in the former convent for private prayer. I was so much more refreshed and ready to teach again after that experience than if we had spent the entire day in meetings.

Desert time is needed throughout the school year as well. Jesus went away from people multiple times. Often, he climbed a mountain to pray. After healing Simon's mother-in-law in the first chapter of Mark's gospel, Jesus is brought many more people to heal. He gets so exhausted that he seeks out solitude.

> That evening, at sunset, they brought to him all who were sick or possessed with demons. And the whole city was gathered around the door. And he cured many who were sick with various diseases, and cast out many demons; and he would not permit the demons to speak, because they knew him.

> In the morning, while it was still very dark, he
> got up and went out to a deserted place, and there he
> prayed. (Mk 1:32–35)

Jesus went off to a "deserted place." Why? Personally, I like to think that Jesus is an introvert like me who likes to be with people and cares about them, but then seriously needs some downtime in order to recharge!

What are some ways that you can get away and recharge? When I have the time and the financial resources, I go to a retreat house. They are usually less expensive than staying at a hotel and you can usually get some spiritual direction and food with the deal. As I mentioned in the introduction, I came up with the idea for this book when I went to a Jesuit retreat house outside of Atlanta for my spring break. I was able to fit in a short visit with my brother and his family who lived in Atlanta at the time as well as a school visit to an Atlanta-area Catholic school, but it was the five days spent on a silent retreat at the Ignatius House that really recharged my teaching batteries.

If you've never made a silent retreat, don't let the *silent* part freak you out. I suggest starting with a weekend silent retreat. These typically begin on a Friday evening and end on Sunday after morning Mass, so it's less than a forty-eight–hour commitment. On top of that, you're not *really* silent the whole time. Usually retreatants are allowed to talk during the Friday welcome dinner, after which they enter into silence until Sunday morning. Typically, you meet with a spiritual director a few times (often Friday night, once on Saturday, and then once again on Sunday), so you do get to talk to another human being. Nonetheless, you still spend most of Saturday quietly, but that's a good thing. It means you get to listen to God! Let him speak to you about the work you're doing. Bring him your concerns about your students, their families, your coworkers, and your boss. Our lives are so busy that we often don't take a moment to hear what God is trying to say to us.

Now you might be thinking, *Well, that's nice, but I don't have time for a weekend retreat or the resources to go away to a retreat center for my spring break.* I get it. I feel fortunate if I get to go on a retreat every few years. However, think about how you might maximize your days off. Can you find a quiet corner or a park where you can set a timer for ten minutes and simply listen to God? Is there a church near you or on your way home from work that has an adoration chapel? Pop in for fifteen minutes and pray a Rosary, or just sit in silence with him.

Another option would be a virtual retreat. This is an online event offered by a retreat house or a spiritual director and can be a great alternative when you can't afford the time or the money for an in-person retreat. One summer I volunteered at Bellarmine Jesuit Retreat House outside Chicago to help them set up their first series of online retreats. These began as evenings of reflection, led by priests, speakers, and spiritual directors. Time for silent prayer and journaling was included between guided prayer and speaker talks. The first of these retreats was led by my friend Becky Eldredge, an author and spiritual director, who offers a whole series of online retreats, including a busy person's online retreat. (So really, even busy people like teachers can find a way to work in at-home retreat times.) Not only do these virtual retreats offer a good option if you don't have a lot of time, but they also don't require any travel expenses. All they require is for you to say to your family that you will not be available for a certain number of minutes, and then find a quiet spot where you can hang a "Do Not Disturb" sign on the door.

Tired of formal prayer time and need a different way to connect with God the Creator? Then go on what author Julia Cameron calls an "artist's date."[10] This comes from her book *The Artist's Way: A Spiritual Path to Higher Creativity*, which I highly recommend for anyone looking to get their creative juices flowing. Don't think that this book is only for painters, actors, and writers. It speaks to us teachers as well because teaching is as much an art as it is a science; thus, we need to tap into our artistic side. Cameron emphasizes that when we create (whether it's art, music, literature—or, I would add, lesson plans!), we are tapping into the Almighty Creator. God is the source of all creation. Therefore, when we create, we are reaching out toward him and partaking in his divine work. Cameron argues that we have to remind ourselves from time to time that creating is really playing. To do that, it's helpful if we take ourselves out on artist's dates.

What exactly is an artist's date? It's a chance for you to be alone with your Creator (not anyone else!) and do something playful. Cameron stresses that you should not take anyone else with you—spouse, children, or friends. If we say that alone time is something that simply can't happen, Cameron urges us to name that as "resistance" (or what we Catholics might call the evil one!) and not to let old "killjoy" rob us of these opportunities.[11] She recommends taking two hours a week (you just gasped, didn't you?) to be by yourself doing anything fun that you love. Maybe it's going for a walk alone. Maybe it's visiting a bookstore and just browsing. Maybe it's going to a museum, a beach, or an old movie theater.

I'm sure many of you are coming up with a million excuses for why this can't or shouldn't or won't happen. I get it. I'm the queen of "forgetting" to do artist's dates, but here's the thing: I've noticed that when I do take an artist's date, I'm happier and more productive than when I don't.

If you are reading this book because you are truly burned out on teaching, I cannot urge you enough to stop what you are doing (before you even read the conclusion), think of one thing you'd really love to do by yourself, and then run to your calendar (or open that app on your phone) and put that artist's date on your schedule within the next seven days.

Do it. Do it now. I'll wait.

Did you do it? If yes, then you may continue reading. If no, stop! For heaven's sake, stop! God is going to meet you there on that date. You don't want to stand him up, do you? Of course not, so commit to that artist's date right now. (And to keep myself honest, I just scheduled a visit to my local botanical garden for a solo stroll through the flowers.)

Now that you've set the date, I really do want you to think about it as time that you and Jesus will spend together. I don't care if you think of your "date" as being with God the Father, or Jesus the ultimate Bridegroom, or the Holy Spirit. I tend to think of these occasions as dates with Jesus, but that might be the old maid in me speaking. If you think of an artist's date as a commitment you are making to both yourself and God, you'll show up! He wants nothing more than to work with you. He loves you. He loves all the hard work you've put into teaching. Invite him into that hard work with you, but also take the time to have fun with him. Those of you who are married know how important it is to take dates with your spouse. Do the same with God. Balance out your relationship with him so that you remember that God is with you in both the good and the bad, in the work and in the play. Seek him out. Let him renew your spirit.

And when you're with him, remember that you don't have to *do* anything special. You just need to *be* with him. Go be with him.

He's waiting for you now.

REFLECTION QUESTIONS

1. In what ways have you practiced servant leadership as a teacher? What challenges and benefits are there to being this kind of leader?
2. How have you seen some of your coworkers teaching simply by example?
3. When and where might you take a spiritual retreat?
4. Where and when are you going on your next artist's date with the Almighty Creator?

Conclusion

As I mentioned earlier, I worked on the outline for this book while on a silent retreat at the Ignatius House Jesuit Retreat Center near Atlanta. For five days, I hiked the beautiful trails that wind through the woods surrounding the retreat house and wandered all the way down to the Chattahoochee River. I sat on benches set high up on cliffs and contemplated the beauty of God's creation. I prayed my way through the outdoor Stations of the Cross and begged God to help me see where I fit into his plan. I met with a spiritual director, I read a book on Ignatian spirituality written by my friend Becky Eldredge, and I sat through many meals in silence.

Some of my favorite times were spent in a room they call the Atrium. This gorgeous room has floor-to-ceiling windows through which you can watch the wildlife in the woods. It's filled with comfy couches and chairs arranged in small groups so that those gathering for non-silent retreats can sit and talk, and those who are on silent retreats can sit quietly by themselves. I spent many hours in this room prayerfully reading the Gospel of Mark, trying to glean wisdom on how I could be a better educator by following Jesus's example as a teacher.

One of my favorite spots to sit in this room was in front of the red-brick fireplace, where a beige loveseat and two green armchairs had been placed. I sat there and read Mark's gospel and jotted down ideas as I went. When I got tired of reading, I plugged in my earbuds, turned on some Matt Maher tunes, and pulled out a Stations of the Cross coloring book I had recently acquired. The coloring craze was in full swing at this time, and the theme of this one seemed appropriate given that I was making the retreat during Lent.

Near the end of the retreat, I sat in one of those green chairs, coloring and listening to Matt Maher. I paused for a bit, like I had done a few times before, and looked up to admire the painting of Jesus that hung above the fireplace. It was like nothing I'd ever seen before. This large square painting sat on the mantel and featured only Jesus's face. The artist's last name, Penley, was painted in white block letters in the lower corner. The background was a bright red brushed with a few broad, dark strokes. Jesus's head seemed to float on a body loosely suggested by more broad strokes, this time golden yellow and gray. The face was bearded, and his dark hair as vaguely defined as his body. Thinner strokes of white and gray depicted the crown of thorns above his head. His eyes were probably the most defined feature of the portrait. They had watched over me each day as I sat and read or wrote or colored.

On this day when I looked up at the portrait, I was a bit startled to realize I had never noticed the crown of thorns before. At this point in my retreat, we had entered Holy Week. You would think between that timing and my Stations of the Cross coloring book, I would have been more attuned to the crown of thorns being there, but I wasn't. Caught up in the sudden realization that this was a picture of Jesus suffering, I felt his eyes gazing on me peacefully and saying, "Did you think any of this was going to be easy?"

What did he mean by "this"? Was he referring to coming up with ideas for my next book? Did he mean teaching? Did he mean following him in general? Any of those could have been possible. His Passion and Death certainly weren't easy, and yet in the midst of his pain, his face was kind, gentle, and strong.

I wanted strength like that. I wanted to endure whatever trials might come my way as an educator with a humility based on kindness and compassion, and a strength that comes from knowing whose you are.

Sometimes, we get assistance through our trials. From time to time, a Veronica might come along who will wipe away our tears for the moment. Other times, a Simon of Cyrene may help us carry our cross for a bit. But in the end, there is no getting around the fact that we must carry our own cross.

An old ad campaign came to mind as I sat there gazing on Jesus crowned with thorns. Perhaps some of you are also old enough to remember it. When I was a child, commercials for the Peace Corps ran often on TV, and they always included the slogan, "It's the toughest job you'll ever love." As a child, I thought, *That's the worst commercial ever! Who likes working hard?*

As an adult, I've come to understand how it's possible to love something that is hard work. In fact, the more challenging a task, the more joy it brings us when we succeed. Easy tasks don't come with as big a payoff.

As I sat in front of the fireplace at Ignatius House, I felt Jesus's love for me and for my fellow educators. As a teacher himself, he surely holds all of us in a special place in his heart. But I also knew Jesus was trying to tell me that teaching is much like joining the Peace Corps.

It's the toughest job we'll ever love.

Acknowledgments

Thanks to my family and friends who have always put up with my grumbling after a rough day of teaching.

Thanks to the students, coworkers, and administrators (past, present, and future) who have given me the opportunity to do the thing God has called me to do.

Thanks to my own teachers and professors—from St. Emily School to St. Viator High School to Marquette University to Northern Illinois University to Loyola University Chicago—you're right on the front lines with me, and you helped me discover the servant leader within me.

Thanks to all my teacher friends from other schools. Hearing your teaching stories always makes me feel better—and often provides some much-needed laughter!

Thanks to the team at Ave Maria Press, especially Lisa Hendey, who first encouraged me to submit a proposal to Ave, and Jaymie Wolfe, my amazing editor who endured long waits on revisions to that proposal as I finished my doctoral degree. (Rule #1 of avoiding teacher burnout: don't pursue your doctorate while teaching full time and trying to write a book. And definitely don't do any of that in the middle of a pandemic.)

Thanks to all my writing friends, especially those in the Catholic Writers Guild and the American Christian Fiction Writers, who have encouraged and inspired me.

AMDG

Notes

1. Linda Darling-Hammond, *Doing What Matters Most: Investing in Quality Teaching* (National Commission on Teaching & America's Future: 1997), 29. https://files.eric.ed.gov/fulltext/ED415183.pdf.

2. Charles M. Payne, *So Much Reform, So Little Change: The Persistence of Failure in Urban Schools* (Cambridge, MA: Harvard Education Press, 2017), 72.

3. John F. Whealon, *Saint Joseph Pocket Edition of the New Testament: In the Good News Translation* (Totowa, NJ: Catholic Book, 2001), 148.

4. Whealon, *Saint Joseph Pocket Edition of the New Testament,* 101.

5. Ron Clark, *The Essential 55: An Award-Winning Educator's Rules for Discovering the Successful Student in Every Child* (New York: Hyperion, 2003).

6. *No Fear Shakespeare: The Taming of the Shrew* (New York: Sparknotes, 2004) act 1, scene 1, line 40.

7. *The Chosen* (TV series), created by Dallas Jenkins, episode 8 (VidAngel, 2019).

8. Nelson Cowan, "History of Hymns: 'Your Grace Is Enough' by Matt Maher," Discipleship Ministries, July 28, 2016, https://www.umcdiscipleship.org/resources/history-of-hymns-your-grace-is-enough-by-matt-maher-1.

9. Linda Darling-Hammond, *The Right to Learn: A Blueprint for Creating Schools that Work*, (San Francisco: Jossey-Bass, 1997), 170.

10. Julia Cameron, *The Artist's Way: A Spiritual Path to Higher Creativity* (New York: J. P. Tarcher/Putnam, 2002), 18.

11. Cameron, *The Artist's Way*, 19–20.

Amy J. Cattapan is a middle school English teacher, speaker, and author who has written or contributed to several books, including *Chicken Soup for the Soul: From Lemons to Lemonade* and the award-winning novels *Angelhood* and *Seven Riddles to Nowhere.* She hosts *Cath-Lit Live!* for the Catholic Writers Guild.

Cattapan has appeared on *The Jennifer Fulwiler Show* on SiriusXM, and *Chicago Catholic.* Her writing has appeared in *Highlights for Children, Hopscotch for Girls, Pockets,* and *Catechist.* She also served as the host for Shalom World TV's *BOOK.ed.*

Cattapan earned a bachelor's degree in English secondary education from Marquette University, a master's degree in instruction for secondary education language arts from Northeastern Illinois University, and a doctorate in curriculum and instruction from Loyola University Chicago. She lives in the Chicago area.

www.ajcattapan.com
Facebook: acattapan
Twitter: @AJcattapan
Instagram: @a.j.cattapan
Pinterest: ajcattapan
YouTube: A.J. Cattapan

AVE
AVE MARIA PRESS

Founded in 1865, Ave Maria Press,
a ministry of the Congregation of
Holy Cross, is a Catholic publishing
company that serves the spiritual and
formative needs of the Church and its
schools, institutions, and ministers;
Christian individuals and families; and
others seeking spiritual nourishment.

For a complete listing of titles from

Ave Maria Press

Sorin Books

Forest of Peace

Christian Classics

visit www.avemariapress.com

AVE MARIA PRESS
Notre Dame, IN
A Ministry of the United States Province of Holy Cross